"It is a joy to know that Dana i: sionate lover of Jesus. Almost a have suffered through the worst terrors this world can throw at them, but whose faith and joy in Jesus remain stronger than the grave. This hope is the most real thing on earth! It is for everyone, in every nation, and I pray every reader of this book will be encouraged to live from the secret place of prayer so that they may also stand in 'the peace of God, which surpasses all understanding' (Philippians 4:7)."

Heidi G. Baker, Ph.D., co-founder and executive chairman of the board, Iris Global

"Do you want a love that burns bright from beginning to end? With specific action steps and thoughtful prayer prompts, *First Love* equips you to say yes to God's invitation to a life marked by confident trust, deep-rooted joy and a love that overflows and impacts all that you do!"

Jodie Berndt, bestselling author, *Praying the Scriptures for Your Children*

"There is nothing more sacred than our heart's flame of first love for Jesus. This book by Dana Candler is the perfect antidote to the epidemic of apathy that constantly threatens our soul's health. Her vulnerability as well as the revelation mined from her own years of pursuit after God's heart is exactly what is needed in our day. I cannot recommend her or this new message enough."

Lee M. Cummings, founding senior pastor, Radiant Church and Radiant Network; author, *School of the Spirit: Living the Holy Spirit–Empowered Life*

"Dana Candler is a deep-hearted lover of Jesus who possesses a deep well of revelation from years spent in intimate conversation with Him. God is speaking to the Church right now about wholehearted communion—with Him and our brothers and sisters. Dana declares these truths with impassioned boldness and clarity. *First Love* will compel you to step headlong into love for God and others at a depth that will prepare you to live wholeheartedly at the end of the ages. I encourage you to read with your Bible open and a pen in hand and allow the Lord to take you into the depths of His love afresh."

Billy Humphrey, director, GateCity Church

"The Bride of Christ worldwide will be praying Song of Solomon 8:6 continually in preparation for the return of her Bridegroom Jesus. Saturated for years in the language and heartbeat of this bridal paradigm, Dana imparts like few others this wisdom and passion in her most timely book, *First Love*."

Lou Engle, president, Lou Engle Ministries

"What kind of wholehearted love does the cross invite? I know no one more capable of guiding our hearts in this quest than Dana Candler. For over twenty years, I've watched her live the message of this book. She shows us that first love is not our destination but rather just the beginning. If you want a burning love for Jesus, this book will strengthen your confidence in the One who—in Dana's words—never starts a fire and walks away."

Bob Sorge, author, *Secrets of the Secret Place*

FIRST
LOVE

FIRST
LOVE

KEEPING PASSION FOR JESUS
IN A WORLD GROWING COLD

DANA CANDLER

Chosen

a division of Baker Publishing Group
Minneapolis, Minnesota

© 2022 by Dana Candler

Published by Chosen Books
11400 Hampshire Avenue South
Minneapolis, Minnesota 55438
www.chosenbooks.com

Chosen Books is a division of
Baker Publishing Group, Grand Rapids, Michigan

Printed in the United States of America

Library of Congress Cataloging-in-Publication Data
Names: Candler, Dana, author.
Title: First love : keeping passion for Jesus in a world growing cold / Dana Candler.
Description: Minneapolis, Minnesota : Chosen Books, a division of Baker
    Publishing Group, [2022] | Includes bibliographical references.
Identifiers: LCCN 2021059211 | ISBN 9780800762568 (trade paper) | ISBN
    9780800762773 (casebound) | ISBN 9781493437474 (ebook)
Subjects: LCSH: God (Christianity)—Worship and love.
Classification: LCC BV4817 .C33 2022 | DDC 248.3—dc23/eng/20220121
LC record available at https://lccn.loc.gov/2021059211

Cover design by Studio Gearbox

Baker Publishing Group publications use paper produced from sustainable forestry practices and post-consumer waste whenever possible.

22 23 24 25 26 27 28   7 6 5 4 3 2 1

To my beloved Matthew: We were in our twenties when we caught a vision to see His beauty, but the decades have taken nothing of the holy aching from your eyes or heart. Run with all your might, me right beside you. We have only seen the edges. . . .

And to Madison, David, Avila and Phoebe: You've been given a great gift in the hour in which you live. When darkness increases, so too will the erupting light of His glory, for all who treasure it. Set your heart with greatest zeal to search and find Jesus as your gold and single passion, and He will set a fire in you that can't be quenched. He who holds the seven stars in His hand holds the fire in your hearts to the end.

CONTENTS

FOREWORD

The landscape of the world today is not what it used to be, and we are never going back to how things were. In an hour when many are focused on self-help, positivity or simply just surviving present tense difficulties, Dana Candler directs our attention beyond: to both the impending storm of increased pressures—in which many believers' hearts will grow gravely cold in their passion for Jesus and love for others—as well as to the magnificent biblical revelation of our ultimate destiny. Jesus is bringing forth His Church to abound in triumphant, tender and unoffendable love.

I believe this book to be one of the most significant books you could read in this hour of history, empowering your present pursuit of Jesus or calling you back from wherever you may have drifted, and giving you the needed path forward in walking in your highest calling: to establish the first commandment—to love the Lord your God with all your heart, soul, mind and strength—in first place in your heart. This important book serves as an arresting rallying cry to the heart of every believer to break any allegiance they have with the snare of lukewarm living and to fervently contend with all their strength to live out their days touching Jesus' passion for them and then burning in an unquenchable love—even through the fiercest testing or trouble.

In nearly fifty years of ministry, I have watched so many start out fiery in their love for God only to gradually lose that fervor, and then accept that loss as an inevitable trajectory of a normal Christian life. If it is not intentionally and zealously fought for, not only will we lose our former devotion to Jesus, but we will be profoundly unprepared and ill-equipped in the very time frame of human history in which God has purposed that we would break forth with the light of victorious love in a dark world.

Our interior life truly is the central subject when it comes to our relationship with the Man Christ Jesus, and our response to Him. What happens deep within our hearts, even where His eyes alone can search and know, determines the course of our days. Jesus said, "Where your treasure is, there your heart will be also" (Matthew 6:21). And the heart, the place in which the wellsprings of life flow, must be zealously kept and guarded (Proverbs 4:23). These are the crucial themes this book focuses on, guiding us into tender and unvarnished conversations with Jesus, if we will allow the full weight of its message to pierce our hearts.

I have known and worked closely with Dana Candler for 25 years and have watched her earnestly set her heart to search out deep things of God's heart, that she might love Him whole-heartedly and consistently. I am delighted to have witnessed her life over the last 25 years, so that I can say she is one of the few I have known who have "stayed with it," embracing the joys and rigors of a life seeking to ever trust and obey Jesus' leadership. Few have written with the sincerity, transparency and genuine conviction over subtle losses of passion for Jesus that Dana communicates. She offers both profound insight and clear direction in this because she has lived it. This is the very sort of radical and loyal responsiveness to the Lord that is needed right now.

The urgency of the times gives witness to the demand for wholehearted givenness to Jesus. It is not time to be halfhearted or casual about the singular most important reality of our lives. It is not the time to assume we are rich and in need of nothing (Revelation 3:16–17), when we are in fact far poorer in our spiritual lives than we comprehend. The vast and lavish banqueting table of intimate fellowship with Jesus and the pleasure of feasting upon the true knowledge of His heart are available to us, but we must each incline our ear to His knock and open the door to Him (Revelation 3:14–22).

I appeal to you as a shepherd in the Body of Christ to read this book several times with a careful responsiveness to the Lord, prayerfully allowing His Spirit to bring the conviction and tenderizing of heart essential for perseverance in victorious love.

I am grateful for Dana's labor to bring this message forth in this critical moment of history we are living. I believe the timeliness of this work to be uncanny, as the stresses and shakings of recent days have made way for an awakening in the hearts of God's people all across the earth. We together as the Body of Christ are in a window of great grace to hear the voice of the Man Christ Jesus calling us by name, arousing us out of our dullness and slumber, that we might enter our destiny of unencumbered affection and full partnership with Him.

My prayer is that through these pages, you will be set on a course, not only of keeping passion for Jesus all your days, but in becoming a friend of the Bridegroom whose joy is made full in Him, delighting in His increase. And that in the days to come, out of your deep intimacy and friendship with Jesus, you would eagerly lift your voice with strength to proclaim His matchless beauty, love and purposes (Isaiah 40:9; John 3:29).

Mike Bickle, International House of Prayer of Kansas City

ACKNOWLEDGMENTS

To every singer, musician and intercessor who has ministered and labored in this little Kansas City house of prayer over the last twenty-plus years: In the monotony of the Midwest and the hiddenness of 24/7 prayer, you have poured out your heart and strength to exalt and adore the name of Jesus, and to cry out in agreement with His promises. Your love offering has come up as a memorial before Him. Thank you for finding His worth and His audience enough and for your lives that offer the anointed atmosphere in which most of these words were written.

Those who gather on Wednesday nights: Somehow in God's profuse kindness, we've come together each week in my living room for well over a decade . . . to study His Word, consider His beauty and strengthen one another in Him. Only the Lord knows how at key times, it's been your prophetic words, your understanding tears, your groans of intercession and your well-timed therapeutic laughter that have served like locked arms on either side of me, keeping my soul steady and injecting fresh faith into my heart whenever it was drawing back. You all are *sisters*, and I'm grateful for you for eternity.

Edie: When I was caught in that span of uncertainty between rawest journal entries and printed words, your voice came to the rescue. To the wrestle of *Should I even release such vulnerable parts of my path to others?* your willingness to personally be touched by each paragraph and then communicate how needed the message was shifted me to believing it was a good thing. Thank you.

Jenna: You carry the same yearning and deep love for Jesus, with a purity and givenness to Him that is truly breathtaking. Thank you for laboring over this book with me, your love for His beauty causing you to care about every syllable.

Mike: Who knows how many thousands would say you have shifted their entire paradigm of the Man Christ Jesus, or how many countless others would say their lives have been changed by the labor of your life: forging night-and-day prayer with singers and musicians when it was unheard of in modernity. But there's something immeasurably precious to me in the gift and honor I've received to walk so closely to you and to see what not everyone sees. Your daily, contagious joy and magnanimity of heart, your carefulness of speech and blessing of those who mistreat you, your devotion to God when no one is looking, and your insatiable love for His Word have all marked me irrevocably. I have such great love and gratitude for you.

INTRODUCTION

When First Love Seems Lost

The pen was slower than it used to be as I tried to push out prayers onto journal pages. Pages that used to fill so effortlessly now stared up at me, bare and cold. I sat alone at the patio table in the quiet of the evening light. Only moments before, I had left town and responsibilities last minute in a frantic need to get away, to slow down, to sit before the Lord in prayer. I couldn't keep going through the motions, feeling as if I were hauling my heart around like deadweight.

Layers of flavors of grief filled my soul, a few identifiable and others more of a mysterious mixture to me. There was the bitter taste of my sadness over the end of an era. It had been almost twenty years of what my husband, Matt, and I had known in the ministry of night-and-day prayer.

Our marriage had been only days old when the International House of Prayer of Kansas City went 24/7, and fresh from the altar, we gladly joined in pioneering that little prayer room, whose aim was to partner in the Great Commission through unceasing songs and intercession, proclaiming the beauty of Jesus and His glorious return.

Now, for nearly two decades, we had labored together with others in the joys, rigors, trials and victories of that mission. This era seemed to close, not because we were leaving or moving on to something new or different, but because many of those with whom we had served and labored through the years *were* and had already moved on themselves.

Although we were championing the next assignment in God for our friends and comrades, the losses were still poignant. To me, it felt as though we had fought and weathered many battles together, all with eyes set ahead on the bigger battles yet to come. Then, just when it felt like we were ready to move into the future with strength, the ranks dispersed. Many of our long-term friends and comrades moved to other cities and assignments, and we were left in the perplexity of wondering how things could possibly continue without them. The International House of Prayer has always been more than a continuous prayer meeting; it is *people*. It is real lives with real families and real hearts that find one another in love with Jesus, intercession and delight in His Word together, who forge a depth in love and friendship that is profound and rich. Our hearts were tearing in this moment of friends moving on. Though we knew our friendships would continue, and we so believed in what God had for them in their next assignments, grief over their going weighed heavy nonetheless.

I found myself looking from side to side in confusion and disheartenment, no longer able to summon the needed energy for the future. Intermingled with that sorrow was the sharp taste of rejection from the email I had received, unannounced. After many years, my contribution was no longer needed for the particular role in ministry that I loved most. Sure, it might not have been said so unfeelingly as that, but it re-spun and obscured my perspective of the past and my vision for the future.

As for the fallouts and difficulties of life, these might seem relatively superficial and insignificant. The truth is, these were a few of the smaller heartaches, together with some greater ones, all barreling in at the same time—all colliding and coalescing into a perfect storm that would lead to an internal fallout I hadn't known before. And the most bitter sorrow wasn't even the circumstances themselves, emotional as they were. Without question, what broke my heart was how things started to break down deep in the secret place of prayer, of intimacy and fellowship with Jesus. This, to me, was the most alarming and upsetting of all.

Like my pen, my heart wouldn't move as it used to in passion for Jesus. My affection for Him felt cooler, though I had fought so hard, over decades now, to stand guard over that holiest communion. It was as though I'd been hovering desperately over a flickering fire when all these external circumstances came stampeding through, while I cupped my hands around the flame, frantically trying to shield it. Yet still the dwindling of this precious flame of affection for Jesus persisted. The love I had at first, what I'd known at times to feel like an all-consuming fire, was undeniably threatened. And the cooling of the fire broke my heart.

Defenses arose quickly to deflect the vulnerable heartache. Self-protecting blame stepped in to guard and board up the aching.

Jesus, it's too much. I found the involuntary prayer escaping from my heart. *All I ever wanted was to love You with my whole heart—and, oh, how this is still my cry—but something happened, and I'm not sure what it was. Somewhere in the middle of all the setbacks, the confusion, the accusations and the discouragement that have accumulated over decades, my heart quit moving as it once did. I did not anticipate the insidious adversaries of my love for You, and somewhere along the way, I lost the brightness of its flame.*

And then the prayer heavy-laden with brokenheartedness and unperceived unbelief: *Jesus, I'm afraid Your call is too impossible. I cannot love You as I did at first—though I want to with all my heart.* Nothing hurts like failing the One you love the most.

The beginnings of this book came from unscripted and vulnerable heartache over dimmed passion and the wrestling with the Lord that followed. I was contending with Him over my heart, which wanted so much to *heed* His call and not lose my first love for Him, yet I found myself incapable of reviving affection and fulfilling that commission (Revelation 2:1–7).

Though I'd set my heart in my youth to love the Lord with all my heart and mind—every step of the way—my resolve and even my careful attention to war against the adversaries of that love were not enough. My devotion to Jesus was painfully genuine, yet nevertheless, bogged down and hindered.

Did I love Jesus with deep sincerity? *Yes.*

Did my love for Him possess the same quality of passion, of hunger, of openhearted trust and confidence that characterized it at first? *No. Admittedly, no.*

The pain and weight of this loss and the sting of my inability to *will* myself into my former passion—to resuscitate a slowed affection—brought my broken, desperate heart into a wrestling with God over His timeless call to His Church: *the call to love Him with everything—and then to keep on loving Him—as we did at first* (Matthew 22:37; Revelation 2:1–7).

God's Commands—Promises of His Enabling Grace

We all have our stories. Each of our hearts carries its own unique history, often with layers of pain and different tastes of disillusionment that have accumulated over time. Life can sneak up on us with struggles that leave us deeply wounded or, at the very least, disheartened. Pressures swell to deafening levels with all the storms and stresses of life. Bills rise. Bodies break. Losses injure. Relationships fail. Is it over? Can our hearts recover their passion? Or for those of us who never had a fiery beginning in Jesus—who don't even know what it is to have our affections laid hold of for Him—is there hope to know His love in this way? Is there such a thing as fiery and fervent love for Jesus no matter what has happened or happens to us? No matter our failures? No matter how distant our hearts feel? And when our hearts are under a damp blanket of coldness and dullness, can they yet burn again?

The Word of God often tells us things that our present experiences radically argue against, yet His Word always wins the argument. When I found myself in this place, with my heart buried in the hurt of circumstances and broken over my weakened passion, I felt as though the Lord tilted my head to see His call to first love, from Revelation 2, at a different angle than I had been viewing it. All I could see was the heaviness of the command and the deficiency of my love. But there was so much I'd forgotten. In a moment, He shifted my perspective with a singular light of new hope: All the commands of God are promises of His enabling grace.

It was as if He came to me where I was—sidelined on the road—and kneeling down to meet me, He invited me with, "When I say, 'Return to first love,' I am not laying a heavy burden on you, but drawing you to *Myself*, your highest Joy and Life. This is not a demand that you are to shoulder, but a call laden with My profuse grace, ready to sweep up the willing heart in its capable wings and transform it into one who overcomes every adversary (Revelation 2:7). This is not the end—not even close. I never start a fire and walk away. There *is* a way forward in My grace. And if you are willing to walk that way with Me, I will cause your heart to come alive in love and joy far beyond what you have imagined is even possible."

It wasn't an inbreaking of light, like a sunrise breaking the night, but rather, it was like a sliver of dim light through a doorway, inviting me to believe and embark on a journey. The

Lord leads in such a way that He always preserves space for our voluntary responses. He is willing to take the time and lead us slowly forward, step by step, our desire intact. He does not force us to come after Him. His call to first love is a fork in the road that requires a response on our part.

Jealously Calling Us Back

It was to the church of Ephesus that Jesus' admonition not to abandon first love came. Jesus had memories of the believers of Ephesus that moved Him. In the early days, about forty years before His words to them were spoken in Revelation, the men and women of the church of Ephesus were known by Him for their love. In the book of Acts, we are told of their history—how the name of Jesus was magnified and how the Word of the Lord grew mightily and prevailed in Ephesus (Acts 19:17–20, 26). The Ephesians' history held stories and testimonies of their full givenness to the Lord, their genuine responsiveness to His Word and their authentic love for Jesus (Ephesians 6:24).

This history was present in Jesus' recollection as He called the Ephesians back to their first love, zealously refusing that they would lose their way in the most primary act of all: *loving Him* (Revelation 2:1–7). After commending them for their works, labor, patience, perseverance and zeal for truth and sound doctrine—an incredible and provoking commendation—He continued with: "Nevertheless I have this against you, that you have left your first love. Remember therefore from where you have fallen; repent and do the first works" (Revelation 2:4–5). Jesus' heart was burdened with something beyond all the ways they were responding externally: He wanted *their hearts involved* and for them to return at the heart level to loving Him *first*.

Jesus could have told the men and women of the Ephesian church that He understood how much they'd been through and how He wouldn't fault them for their loss of fervency, but

He didn't. Instead, He spoke of their first love as something invaluable that they had started with and were never to have abandoned along the way. Rather than accepting their other virtuous qualities and actions as cause to overlook the dwindling of their first love, Jesus essentially rendered all the other things *valueless* without the undergirding fire of affection they began with. Their first works were fueled by *first love*, making them altogether different than the works now being offered. A different mixture of motivation had set in, esteeming these works unsalable to Jesus (1 Corinthians 13:1–3). The loss was such that Jesus called them to *repent* for departing from it and to *return* to what they did at first—works motivated and sustained by their love for Him—or else He would remove their lamp entirely. In other words, He would rather extinguish their lamp completely—their favor and outward impact—than allow them to maintain an external witness not fueled by inward love.

It might be easy for us to assume this was to a specific church in the apostle John's day, that Jesus wasn't necessarily speaking to His Church in general and in modernity. Yet the Word of God is not this shortsighted, and what Jesus spoke in the letters to the churches is ageless in its message and all the more poignantly relevant as the events surrounding His return draw near.

This is how essential and imperative *first love* in His people is to Jesus. In our proneness to prioritize external impact over intimacy with Him, it is something worthy of the careful consideration of our hearts. His message to Ephesus is a timeless statement to His Church, reflecting His unchanging heart, purpose and desire. He holds memories of each one of us, of the fire He ignited within us in the beginning and the early devotion so precious to Him. He wants love for Him to fuel our every word and deed, and when He does not find this sequence from inward love to outward light in us, He jealously calls us back.

Did the church of Ephesus return to its first love? We don't know for sure, but it seems highly probable from Church history that they *did not*.

When we have lost our earlier passion for the Lord, or have never known it, will we respond to Jesus' appeal to first love? A thousand things will keep us convinced to choose the path of just settling in and justifying any diminished fervency, stunted affection or cautionary distance. Yet the light in the doorway beckons. There *is* another way. It's the way to life and joy and openhearted trust. He would not have asked it of us if He did not have full provisions of grace ready to give flight to our voluntary choice.

Jesus entreats us to walk willingly through the door and to follow Him on the journey. He invites us to embrace the humility that trusts, even when we don't see the possibility. His Word is true and does not lie. His commands are not burdensome when the grace of God is the strength of our lives.

Keeping first love for Jesus *is possible*. And when it gets sidelined or grows dim, renewed burning passion is the future of any who are willing to heed His voice and respond to His grace.

Let us follow the light of His Word, the truth that confronts our untruths, and embrace the steps He has laid out before us until our hearts are no longer deadweight but flowing and alive—until we burn with His passion for us and our responsive passion for Him. This is the exchange He gave His life to purchase and to receive from our willing hearts.

As we take each step forward, the voice of the One who both ignites and rekindles the human heart—the One who spoke light into darkness in the beginning—now speaks over our limp and dwindled love, "Heart, soul, mind and strength—come alive!"

Hearing Jesus Call Us to First Love

We sat there on the floor, facing one another in wonder, just taking each other in, it all hitting us in waves simultaneously. When he finally spoke, it was only to confirm what our hearts and eyes had already been communicating: *So this is what you look like. I've waited for you, prayed for you, wondered what you'd be like, and here you are.*

I don't think I could pinpoint the exact moment I fell in love with Matt Candler, but I could spend hours describing the first days, weeks and months of our relationship. The vulnerability, lovesickness-when-apart, openheartedness and wonder are etched in full color and emotion in my memory as if it were yesterday. The written words on pages, the endless hours of conversations, the laughter, the tears. He was everything I'd ever hoped for and everything I never knew I needed all in one.

I remember the overwhelming feeling of trying to catch him up—and he me—on 22 years of life, the years we'd missed of each other's lives prior. Separated by geography, we spent our driving hours to meet each other—crisscrossing Missouri and Oklahoma—with a tape recorder in hand, recounting all the old stories we could think of from our childhoods, our youth, our families, our pains and our joys—everything that had formed who we were. We wanted each other to know it all, to receive the whole package and the whole story. Newly in love, we wanted to know one another fully as we ran arm in arm into the future together.

First Love in Christ

What is first love? We know it intuitively, what it means and what it looks like, even if we've never tried to put it into words or never experienced it in a personal way. First love is notorious for its contagious joy and exuberance and its passionate, uninhibited nature. When love is new and freshly awakened, wonder and delight are abundant, desire is full, sacrifice and striving are foreign concepts, and full givenness, one to another, is the only conceivable way to live. *Our first love for the Lord is no exception.*

There's nothing in the world that can compare with the awakening of the human heart to the beauty and love of Christ—the arising passion in the wake of catching sight of and being overcome by His great love for us. No other experience in all of life is equal to when the Lord comes and arrests our affections by His Spirit—winning them over to Himself—by giving us a taste of His kindness and a glimpse of His majesty (Romans 5:5). In these awakenings, He stirs us to peer into the vast mystery of His love for us, opening the eyes of our hearts to see the One "in whom are hidden all the treasures of wisdom and knowledge" (Colossians 2:3). He awakens hunger through the tasting and draws us into a seeking by giving us a glimpse (1 Peter 2:2–3).

When the Lord stirs first love in us like this, we are never quite the same. When He rushes in to fill the innate inward ache of the human soul with the only fulfillment that can answer and satisfy, we are changed. He who has seen Jesus cannot unsee Him, and she who has tasted cannot forget the sweetness.

Something at the deepest level has taken place. An irrevocable exchange has transpired, and we've been marked by Him forever. He wins us to Himself here in ways that are far more strategic than we might have imagined. After all, first love is not meant by the Lord to be just a fiery beginning that fades out with time. It is to be the *first fire* and catalyst of a love that only increases in its strength, passion and devotion through all the seasons of our lives . . . until we see the Lord.

> He who has seen Jesus cannot unsee Him, and she who has tasted cannot forget the sweetness.

Whenever there is a waning, a loss, a tempering of fervency, it is to serve as the spark that ignites the fire once again. First love is never to be the high point, followed by a declining trajectory, but rather it is the necessary starting point for a love that continues to increase and abound in His grace.

First Fire to Fuel the Future

My early days of loving Jesus, when He won me over with His unrelenting love, evidenced a strong passion for Him. I was simply overcome by a God who desired more than a relationship of function or legal position with His people. He longed for a relationship of deep affection. He is a Bridegroom God who had profound tenderness toward me and desired closest relationship and partnership with *me*.

In my early twenties, having known the Lord all my life prior, I experienced something in Him unlike anything I had yet encountered. It was as if the love of Christ broke through to a greater depth than ever before, reaching the inner places of my heart and soul, getting beneath all my performing, all my arguments, all my resistances, down to the hidden and most vulnerable parts of me. His love won me over. Grace broke through to my inner being in a way it never had before. Overwhelming worship followed as I marveled that He loved me personally, profoundly, invasively. I was undone by it, irrevocably undone.

In the wake of such love, I responded with all my heart. With vision clear of any fog that seems to settle without warning over time, sheer joy over the treasure I had found in Him compelled me forward. Vows to be faithful and true were easy, and denying self was effortless and heartfelt. I made bold, earnest promises to love Him entirely, without reservation, until I saw Him face-to-face.

Such fervor and strain-free strides were not wrong, but *exceedingly right*. They were first love in motion—a wholehearted loving of the One who loved me first (1 John 4:19). Though I was admittedly naïve as to how fierce the battle and the opponents, and how robust the perseverance required, the level to which His love laid hold of me and then my corresponding wholehearted response to Him were the necessary beginnings for the sustenance of that very love. And Jesus knew it all along. He knows it with each of us.

The fire of passion He ignites in us at first is part of His knowing the future testing and struggles. He knows how exceedingly dependent we must become upon Him—a slow dying to our own self-strength—in order that we might fulfill those early vows. He knows His purpose in our lives is not just the maintaining of early affection, nor the surviving of faith. It goes far beyond merely subsisting. Jesus zealously purposes that our faith and love come through the testing of fire like gold, abounding more and more, and be found to praise, honor and glory at His coming (Philippians 1:9; 1 Peter 1:7). He knows His full intention to finish the good work He began in us and to bring each of us forth into victorious love as we respond to Him and partner with Him in this glorious call (Philippians 1:6).

The Zeal of the Lord to Bring Forth Love

At the heart of all that we are and all that we do is a Person: the Man Christ Jesus, who is the Lord seated at the right hand of God the Father. The inward fire of our intimacy with Him is the center of everything—both individually and corporately as His Church. He didn't always have a human frame. He was from everlasting, but in the fullness of time He came and wrapped Himself in garments of flesh. Amid mostly scorned love, He set His face like flint and went to His death on the cross. He gave His life for us that He might bring us to God. He died. He rose. He ascended. He sat down at the right hand of the Majesty on high, with a future and a plan ahead of Him. There He sits, that pulsating, consuming, impassioned heart—seated there only for a time, until the day He returns and commences the restoration of all things and "the day of the gladness of His heart" (Song of Songs 3:11).

Peter said: *Having not seen Him, you love Him* (1 Peter 1:8). We love a real Person, and that love is the central passion of all we are. He wants the hearts of His people—those whom He has ransomed back to Himself—to receive and abide in His love and to respond voluntarily with an all-consuming, fervent devotion.

The Father desires to give His Son the inheritance of a Church that loves the Son of God with a wholehearted love, a Bride who unreservedly agrees with Him in all that He is and all that He does and will do. He wants a Church that gives witness with the whole of their hearts and lives: *All that You are is beautiful*. His purpose is to shine in the hearts of His people, to give us "the light of the knowledge of the glory of God in the face of Jesus Christ" (2 Corinthians 4:6), so that with every increasing measure of knowledge, we would have a simultaneous increase in our love for Him. That the Church would not love the Lord with fractions, but in fullness. That His Bride would not pick and choose and only embrace parts of Him, but that our love would abound for Him in every aspect of who He is.

Jesus wants His Church to live perpetually in an ardent, joyful loyalty to Himself. He is not after a lukewarm, indifferent, divided love—or a love that started fiery and becomes tempered over time. He gave all for the gut-level, wholly devoted love of His Bride, the Church, the worthy love befitting the love He demonstrated for her. He wants our deepest affections.

In John 17, Jesus prayed that the very love with which the Father loved Him would be in us. Paul picked up on this prayer—specifically for the church of Ephesus—in Ephesians 3, praying for rooting and grounding in the love of Christ, the comprehension of His love, in all its vastness. The words of Jesus in Revelation are perhaps the most unfiltered and straightforward of all. Jesus pleaded that we would persevere and keep our first love for Him alive until He comes (Revelation 2:4).

Jesus demands a love that burns bright from beginning to end. He calls us to love Him with all our heart, soul, mind and strength and then demands that we never lose that wholehearted, fervent devotion. The Father has no intention of offering His Son a dull and disconnected church as His inheritance. The Son will return to a fervent Bride, from every tongue and tribe and nation, who loves Him with the entirety of her existence (Revelation 19:7; 22:17). He wants a Church living in the grace and fervency of *first love* all the way to the end.

Jesus is fully invested in us. We are His inheritance, and He has full intention of keeping our love alive for Him—that He might present us to Himself pure and spotless (Ephesians 1:18; 5:27). He did not descend from His glory and endure the affliction of dying for us only to culminate in a lukewarm flame of love—cooled by all the difficulties and cares of life. He has zeal that our passion for Him would not only survive, but that it would *thrive* until the day we see Him face-to-face. The biblical story does not end with a fainting church, but with the people of God knowing who they are and prepared as His Bride, filled with a consuming love for Jesus and crying out for His return (Revelation 19:7; 22:17).

Because His leadership is perfect, His plan is sure and His heart is always engaged, Jesus never settles in and leans back with us in our waned passion, accepting it. To do so would be to leave us in a way of life beneath what He desired for us and less than our holy destinies in Him—what He gave His life to provide for us. Thus, His call to His Church to keep first love is not overreaching, but fitting. Furthermore, His expectation that we heed Him in this call is not too demanding, but perfect and right.

The Difficulty of the Call

This is where most of us halt. It's in the difficulty with His call. We sign off relatively easily on the possibility of loving Him to the end in a general sense—just like any marriage vow promises to love to the end. Yet His call goes deeper and is far more extensive than this. He not only wants us *generally* to love Him all of our days, but He wants us to love Him with *entirety* and *full fervency* until the day *we see Him face-to-face*.

His call to love Him with everything is truly the first and greatest commandment; thus, the continuous fight to have and keep Him first in our affections is undeniably the highest and worthiest battle of our lives (Matthew 22:36–40). Yet the adversary makes his aim straight at the heart, and the threats to that love are countless along life's path. Confusion hits. Doubts assail. Unbelief hovers. Betrayals level. And the gravity weighs heavy upon us as the years and difficult circumstances unfold one by one. Without realizing it, what began as a heart-wide-open, fully abandoned responsiveness to Jesus can subtly wane and even wither away over time if we do not continually cultivate and persevere in it.

As the years have transpired in my life, so too have the disappointments, the piling up of the accusations from the accuser and from my own heart, the exposing of my own shortcomings and deficiencies, the pain and confusion of unforeseen twists and turns. This unfolding of life and circumstances is foreign to no one as we sojourn forward in following Jesus. We might almost expect the Lord to back off from His insistence on keeping our first love for Him. Such a demand in the face of legitimate disheartenment can feel unreasonable. His adamancy in this can strike our hearts as though He's out of touch. Yet He does not relent, continuing to insist upon our full fervency and entire devotion, irrespective of what unfolds in our lives. To demand less would not be love. This is not His being unreasonable. No, it's simply His being unwilling to deny us our full inheritance and His full inheritance in us. We were made for wholehearted love, and He refuses to relent in establishing that in us.

> **We were made for wholehearted love, and He refuses to relent in establishing that in us.**

Keeping First Love Is Possible

I never planned for anything to change in my fervency and passion for Jesus. Maybe I was like Peter, sure that even if all the others left the Lord, I wouldn't—sure that mine would be the passion that would endure (Matthew 26:35). Yet even when we watch over our hearts with all diligence, even when we are faithful to war against and overcome some of the giants that shut down love—such as offense and bitterness—there are still many subtle thieves seeking to creep in and steal (Proverbs 4:23).

Misunderstanding confounds. Discouragement lurks. Weariness born of the weight of being accused day after day takes its toll. Sometimes it's not the adversaries that come through the front door, but the enemies that sneak in silently through the cracked-open windows of our souls. These move in stealthily and incrementally, overtaking our love for Jesus. It can feel as though it's over—like we'll never love Jesus with wholehearted, untainted passion again. But this perspective shortchanges and greatly underestimates the leadership and power of Jesus.

This trajectory of waning passion is real and mournfully common in God's people, but that does not mean it is inevitable or what we should expect from the heart that loves Him. Our assumptions must be confronted and renewed by the truth of the Gospel and all that the New Testament claims as the *normal* course for the heart and lives of those in Christ. And the testimony of Scripture should provoke us into the wrestling over our own hearts, the crying out and contending with the Lord that ours would be the trajectory put forth by Scripture, that we would love Him with an abounding love and walk in a path that burns brighter and brighter until the perfect day (Proverbs 4:18; Philippians 1:9–11).

His Love Is Our Love's Source

This is where we need to hear the words of Jesus with fresh faith. His perspective here is, in fact, opposite of ours. We start with our circumstances and heartaches and conclude that they are too much for love to continue as it once did. Or perhaps we start with our limp love, uncertain of when and where something got in to decrease the flame, and we look at Him despairingly, brokenhearted that we could not keep our promise to love Him as we had vowed. His starting point, rather, is not with our circumstances or our dimmed love, but with *His love* and the power of His affection, as He demonstrated in His own self-giving on the cross. With this beginning point, He concludes there is no circumstance or power—not even death itself that can come close to overpowering the strength, the breadth and the encompassing fire of His love (Romans 8:35–39; Ephesians 3:16–19).

He does not view His love on one side of a scale and our troubles on the other, like equal forces dueling it out over the heart. Rather, the perspective of Jesus and the testimony of Scripture hold that many waters cannot quench His love, that floods cannot drown it out and that *our love for Him* proceeds not from ourselves, but from this inexhaustible source and fountain (Song of Songs 8:6–7; 1 John 4:10).

Our circumstances and heartache and dullness are real, but they are not stronger or more powerful than His love. Thus, in this call not to abandon our first love, He opens the vast treasury of His infinite grace to us, calling us to fight against the adversaries and lay hold of the testimony He desires to give us: that is, keeping our first love all our days.

The passion and loyalty of our *early love* for God—that all-in, joyful, heart-on-the-line, vulnerable givenness—that love that came in the wake of being stirred and overcome by His own love for us, are essential and strategic to our continued fervency. He wants that early love to last from the beginning of our days to the end, no matter what we face in all the struggles of life that follow. In fact, it is this unquenchable love that is to sustain us and make us more than conquerors through every trial and hardship we face (Song of Songs 8:6–7; Romans 8:35–39). He doesn't deem it as something we will inevitably lose, but as something we must *vehemently guard* every step of the way, something we must continually cultivate and keep and abide in, something that will be the very source of our victory (John 15:9).

First love, then, with its distinctive qualities, was never meant to be *first* love, but simply *love*. And *love* is always to carry those primary attributes of openhearted trust, wholehearted givenness, overflowing joy and vibrant affection toward God. Circumstances change, seasons cycle through, life plays out, bodies age and break down—disappointments, trials and troubles come—but love is always to remain alive and passionate. In fact, first love is not only something the Holy Spirit wants to maintain in us but also something He wants to *increase* in us.

We're not just to hold on to the love we began with and seek to keep that the standard, but rather our love is to abound still more and more. In our fallenness and from our own resources, it is impossible to fulfill such a trajectory; yet we do not look to our own resources. One of the primary jobs of the Holy Spirit is to enable us to love God wholeheartedly and to empower us not only to love as we did at first, but to love *more and more*, until we finally see Him, that His joy would both remain in us and be made full (John 15:11; Philippians 1:9–11).

First in Both Priority and Quality

To Jesus, it was only a short time ago that He spoke to His servant and friend John on the island of Patmos and gave him the message the book of Revelation makes known—a message not only to believers alive in John's day but also to the believers in every generation (2 Peter 3:8; Revelation 1:1). What He spoke to John are timeless truths of what He desires and values, a message only made even more essential as His return draws nearer and the challenges His Church faces increase. His message to Ephesus about first love echoed what He proclaimed as He walked the earth and what He demonstrated by His dying: He wants our ardent affection.

He does not want partial love from His people, but *full passion*. Jealous for our *all*, He refuses that His Church should offer Him a surface-level devotion. Just as He is not distant and indifferent to us, but profoundly engaged with every response of our hearts, every detail of our lives, He desires and calls for this same kind of wholehearted, tender love and responsiveness from His people.

The Father will offer His Son a fervent, wholehearted people as His glorious inheritance. The Son will return to a Church that is abounding in great love for Him and living in expectant yearning for His return. He desires for His Church to live perpetually in passionate, joyful, fully trusting love. He gave *all* for the gut-level, wholly loyal, self-giving, full-trusting love of His Bride—the Church. His Word promises that He will return to a Bride who loves Him with a fervent and holy love (1 Corinthians 1:7–9; Ephesians 5:27; Revelation 19:6–9; 22:17).

The heart of Jesus implores us for first love—*first,* speaking both of *priority* and of *quality.* He wants our love for Him to be the preeminent aim of our lives and reward of our hearts— that we would love Him with all our heart, all our soul, all our mind and all our strength (Matthew 22:37). When He calls us to first love, He calls us to the great commandment to love Him with all that we are, without division and with full givenness. Furthermore, this admonition of Jesus to return to first love also speaks of our love for Him perpetually carrying the qualities of our earliest days—when our hearts were first awakened and stirred by His Spirit in love and devotion.

We need first love, both at the beginning and all the way to the end. So whether we find ourselves longing to be awakened for the *first time* with the immeasurable, unrelenting love of Christ, or we are sitting sidelined in disheartenment along life's path, unsure when it was that we lost the openhearted passion we once had for Him, Jesus is inviting us to draw near to Him. We were never fashioned to live without a heart alive in passion for Jesus, and He desires to give us grace to walk in that passion—from beginning to end.

Jesus, knowing every opponent and every possible challenge that would beset us in our greatest calling of loving God *first*, promises us abundant grace to love Him every step of the way with the same yearning, trusting, believing, confident love that we had in the earliest days. He did not stir our hearts with first love and then leave us to ourselves. Rather, He lit a fire of affection in us by His love and gave us a taste of His beauty as a means of persevering in the warmth of passion all our days.

> **Embers are not endings to Him—but new beginnings.**

Though seasons and difficult circumstances and setbacks will test our love, they do not have to strip it of its fire. He wants us not only to conquer but also to *more than conquer* the adversaries of love (Romans 8:37). He is the keeper of the flame, and wherever He finds a willing heart, He will stir the fire once again. Embers are not endings to Him—but new beginnings.

However, in order to go forward we must first *return*.

PRAYER

Jesus, I set the eyes of my heart upon You right now. You are the One seated upon the throne at the right hand of the Father. You are alive and Your heart burns with everlasting desire and zeal for Your full inheritance of wholehearted love in the hearts of Your people. I turn my heart and attention toward this desire and call. I incline my ear to hear Your voice and Your heart, speaking to me of how You want first love in me. I say "yes" to Your stirring, to the awakening of fresh hunger and desire by Your Spirit in me. I ask You to lay hold of my heart more and more as You lead me forward in loving You with all my heart, soul, mind, and strength and in keeping passion for You all my days.

STEPS FORWARD IN KEEPING PASSION FOR JESUS

* Our first step forward in keeping passion for Jesus is turning our attention to hear His call, taking to heart the fact that He wants our first love.

* Next, we set our hearts to believe by faith He will give us immeasurable grace to walk in it and keep it.

* Then, we tell Jesus we are willing to stir our hearts with responsiveness to His fiery love. Take a few minutes right now to acknowledge your desire to turn your attention to Jesus and express your heart to Him using the prayer above or your own words.

Returning to the Bridegroom Who Loved Us First

t was Jesus' jealousy that broke me. Until I saw His jealousy over me, I kept up a guard even from the good news of His affection and passion for His people—for *me*.

It was the fall of 1998, and I sat in the back of a classroom at Grace Training Center Bible School in Kansas City, a few years after that day at eighteen when I'd hugged my parents good-bye and braved the new horizon of on-my-own. With new friends few and old friends far, I can't help but taste the loneliness I felt sitting in that chair. Even so, what I didn't know was coming was a closeness to Jesus that I'd never known, all beginning as I listened to class after class, taught by a man named Mike Bickle, about the passion of Jesus for His Church, His Bride, as revealed in the Song of Solomon. And though leaning in, I initially still held on to an arms-crossed hesitation.

It all seemed too good to be true. In my wrestle, I contemplated that if indeed these things *were* true about Jesus and His heart for His people, it was going to really mess me up.

Performance dies a slow death, waffling back and forth on its two self-rooted sides—striving and condemnation—only surrendering when something stronger breaks its power. That's what happened to me when the Lord won me over by His love. I was twenty years old when I saw something so fierce in Him that it humbled me into weeping acceptance. It broke the back of unperceived areas of performance and set me free of subtle patterns of seeking to earn, striving to attain and coming up short in self-condemnation. He loved me so fiercely, so intensely, so unrelentingly that my efforts would never be great enough or deficient enough to stand at the helm and be in control. That's the day I truly met the Bridegroom. That's the day He truly won me with His love. That's the day *grace broke through to my gut*.[1]

Suddenly, this subtle pattern of relating to God based upon my own efforts became unraveled by a love that was stronger than my highs of passion and deeper than my lows of self-condemnation, a holy love that refused to allow me to bring any more to the table—good or bad.

His love wrestled with my arguments and triumphed. His passion reduced me to the truth of my unworthiness and yet crowned me with undeserved, unrelenting affection. He loved me *because He loved me*, and His was a love and redemption based not on my deserving, but entirely on Himself and out of His own splendid character and personality (Deuteronomy 7:7). He loved me *first* (1 John 4:19).

And there in my raw, reduced state, before His self-giving, undeserved love, my eyes were opened in amazement and admiration to the vast majesty of Jesus—how gloriously beautiful He was in His heart, His emotions, His personality, His plan and His story. I was overcome by His profound tenderness and fierce love for me, delighting in me even in my weakness and immaturity.

Jesus asked of me only what He Himself had already given: *wholehearted love* (Matthew 22:37). He was jealous for it and would accept nothing less. He didn't want my efforts of trying to earn something. He wanted my aching, my affection and all of my actions to break forth as holy responses to this love and grace, undeserved and unmerited. Any effort or action not propelled forth from this burning center of love—born from His own preceding love—was only empty, clanging noise to Him (1 Corinthians 13:1; 1 John 4:19). He wanted my deep affection, my continual fellowship and my partnership with Him—the worthy calling of every believer.

The combination of His beauty and love tore open in me a depth of hunger and desire for Him I'd never known before. I wanted to know everything about Him. I wanted to give my life to Him in every way: heart, soul, mind and strength. It brought forth a different kind of resolve to love Him in return—a resolve of passion and desire, bursting forth from the Lord's *own* passion and desire. Out of the overwhelming overflow of His love and intimate knowledge of me, I vowed to love the Lord with all my heart, soul, mind and strength. To know Him deeply became what I wanted more than anything. I loved Him because He first loved me (1 John 4:19).

Somehow, the understanding of such a holy affection in Him brought light and exposed many ways that my confidence was still rooted in my own strength and the power of my own love. The Lord began to rework my confidence, to make its foundation not in my own zeal or strength but in His ardent affection and faithful leadership. My heart began to resonate with what that old hymn proclaims: "Could my zeal no respite know, Could my tears forever flow . . . Thou must save and Thou alone. . . . Nothing in my hand I bring. Simply to the Cross I cling."[2]

As never before, I began to look to His cross and the flame in His heart that brought Him to that cross as the place where I should hinge my assurance. He, not I, was at the helm of my devotion.

During this conversion of confidence, I spent hours journaling, tears streaming, essentially becoming inwardly rewired by the truths of God's tenderness with me in my weakness, His passion for all of my affection and His deep delight in me personally, whom He had fashioned. These truths did, in fact, "mess me up" in a most holy way. And I never recovered. In that time, I wrote these words:

Jealous Love
Little mountain, what are you?
Little ocean, where lies your strength?
If the hand that formed the universe holds my heart,
How can man or power take me from Him?
His love leaves the oceans small
And the mountains powerless to separate.
The One that loves me
Will not surrender me to another hand
Though all of hell stands in His way.
He will have me.
He will keep me.
He will not give me over to any other.
I had thought that I could lose my way
Until I remembered jealousy keeps me.
He keeps me,
And I'm a fool to think another could steal
What He has called His own.
If the Consuming Fire is ravished by my small heart,
What man of the earth,
What power of heaven or hell,
Can keep me from Him?
No mountain He would not conquer;
No sea He would not cross.
Foolish I was to fear that all could be lost.
My heart is not kept by my own love,
But by the River of love from His heart.
I am my Beloved's, and He is mine.

Returning to the Tender Love of Christ

The love of Christ is different than any other. He loved us while we were still His enemies, and He gave His life in death to save us while we were yet afar off. He loved us first. Before we responded. Before we turned to Him and received and believed in Him. Before our own hearts began to love. He loved us. Thus, when He calls us back to remember and return to that love we had at first, inherent in His call is a returning and a remembering of His love, His delight, the tasting again of His unmerited affection that was first the awakener of our hearts. His call back to first love is first a call back to Himself—the One who loved us first. It is a coming back to the all-consuming flame of His passion, to drink again of the fountain of His delight, receiving and believing with the same openheartedness and receptivity as we did at first (1 John 4:16).

To start with, our response would be to stop short at the true starting point. Our love for Him is only a *response* to His great love for us. He beckons us to the place of opening our hearts to His enjoyment and delight over us, the place of confidence—where we know our belovedness to Him and take to heart His pleasure over us. This is not something from which we ever move on. It is the essential starting point, and unless we go back to that beginning, unless our joy is restored there, we will end up off course. That hidden place of fellowship with Him and confidence in His delight in us is the crucial heartbeat for our every movement forward. He is the One who loved us and gave His life for us. We love Him because He first loved us.

For me, in a looming crisis of waned passion, without even the ability to diagnose where the fallout was or to locate the cause for the slow extinguishing, His call was to come face-to-face with His jealous love once more. I might have drifted from earlier passion, but the divine jealousy that once left my arguments speechless and my striving powerless had not changed, had not dwindled, had not diminished in the smallest degree. What marked me irrevocably in my youth was what I needed to mark me once more, decades later, and repeatedly into my future. It is for us all. We are to return to *Him*, to be humbly and piercingly crushed once more under the weight of the Gospel—of His tender love and grace.

> **What marked me irrevocably in my youth was what I needed to mark me once more, decades later, and repeatedly into my future.**

Condemnation is a thief, and how easily we let it rob us. We can unwittingly assign our disappointments with ourselves to the Lord, assuming He carries the same disappointed view that we carry of ourselves. Nothing disempowers the heart more. From here, He calls us back. Back to Himself. Back to His heart. Back to His unchanging and unyielding, jealous love. It's as though He steps in and says to me—to you:

So, you grew up, and you changed, and thus you believe I have too. But I was already old and unchanging—the Ancient of Days, the same yesterday, today and forever. Do you think I became subject to your highs and lows? To your flighty passion or dimming affection? To your proneness to loss of fervency? Do you think I rise and fall with you? Do you think I am as surprised by your inconsistency of devotion as you are? No.

Before you were formed, I knew you. I knew your path and the steps you would take. I knew how the circumstances would twist and turn, leaving you surprised and confused at times. I knew.

I knew the sincerity of your love in the beginning, and I knew My own jealousy to bring it forth to completion in you, My inheritance. I am as jealous as I have been from the first day, and I see far more than you see of yourself. I saw it from your mother's womb—the end from the beginning. And I have not changed My mind. You are Mine!

Will you believe Me? In the rising and falling of your own deficiencies, will You cling to Me and trust My zeal more than your own? Will you continue in the simplicity of devotion and sincerity of heart toward Me, your confidence rooted not in yourself but in Me? Will you keep your heart open and vulnerable to Me, not walling up when you discover your weakness . . . not distancing yourself, but clinging to Me every step of the way? Will you love Me as you did at first? Because I have always loved you as I did at first. Will you take this love of Mine into the most secret place of Your heart and there abide in it?

The Bridegroom Calls Us Back

Jesus is the most wholehearted Person alive. He created and redeemed us with the deep passion and tender mercy of a husband (Isaiah 54:5). And when we hear Jesus calling us back to first love in Revelation 2, both to His Church corporately and to us individually, He is appealing to us from His identity as the Bridegroom and urging us to respond as His Bride.

A parallel passage to Jesus' call to first love in Revelation 2 is Jeremiah 2, when the Lord spoke to Israel: "I remember you, . . . the love of your betrothal, when you went after Me in the wilderness" (v. 2). Just as He appealed to Israel to return to the tender beginnings of trust, abandonment and love for Him, now in one of the final chapters of the written Word, He calls His Church—Jew and Gentile alike—to come back to first love and respond to Him as the betrothed Bride that we are, with wholehearted and joyful devotion.

Jesus has always been, and will always be, the Bridegroom. The biblical story that began with a marriage ends with a wedding. It opens with a foreshadowing in Genesis 2 and culminates with the fulfillment at the marriage supper of the Lamb

(Genesis 2:21–24; Ephesians 5:32; Revelation 19:6–9). From the opening of the story in the Garden, like an arrow shot straight through the bleeding hearts of the prophets, all the way to the dawning of the incarnation—when the Son Himself left His throne to come in the flesh and give His life as a ransom for us—*He was the Bridegroom.*

This great story is not of a man and woman, but of Jesus, the divine Bridegroom, and the beautiful corporate Bride—redeemed humanity—brought out of scorn and separation and brought forth as the beloved Bride, the crowning inheritance of Jesus! And all the way to the finale of the story, He is leading human history and maturing His Church to this glorious end.

I believe Jesus intended for the Good News of the Gospel to be heard with the sound of the Bridegroom-Maker in its call, ever beckoning us to Himself with tenderness and jealous love (Isaiah 54:5). Through His servant Paul, He placed this understanding at the very heart of the Gospel by revealing His death on the cross as that of the Bridegroom giving His life for His Bride (Ephesians 5:28–31). He pleaded through His parables: "It's like a wedding! Don't make light of it!"—urging us never to get distant and passive, but to live as a betrothed bride whose wedding day is ever present in her thoughts and whose time and energy are all focused and directed toward that momentous day ahead (Matthew 22:5).

He warned of the delay before the wedding and the wisdom of acquiring oil so that our lamps would continue burning until He comes. He emphasized the need for watchfulness to counteract the strong pull toward passivity and discouragement as the delay spans wide (Matthew 25:5). As the Bridegroom, He spoke of the time when He would be taken away and of the only fitting response His friends would offer in that absence: *They would long for His return* (Matthew 9:15).

Jesus is the jealous Bridegroom who gave His life for us, and refuses dormant love from us, and we are that chosen inheritance of the Lamb, purchased and redeemed, that He might present us to Himself in splendor on the day of the gladness of His heart, the glorious day (Ephesians 5:25, 27; Revelation 19:7).

The relationship between Christ and the Church, which Paul described in the context of marital love, he called a great mystery. God chose that this picture would capture the delight and exclusivity that Christ feels for His Church. He desires that we relate to Him in His jealousy and tenderness toward us, establishing a confidence in us that flows from knowing intimacy with Him and His enjoyment over us. Through the cross, we are reconciled to God and made fully righteous. As the Bridegroom sees His Bride through this lens of righteousness and holiness, His heart is stirred with affection (2 Corinthians 5:18, 21).

With holy zeal and a deep tenderness more powerful than the strongest man's resistance, He calls us by name to return to a full love, a full trust and a full fidelity to Him. My love for Him is not an insignificant thing to Him. Your love for Him is not minor to Him. And our history in Him—the fire of love He lit within us—is not something He is willing to let dwindle into a former affection.

As the end of the ages culminates, the Lord will bring this revelation of His identity as Bridegroom to great centrality, known and experienced both corporately and personally in the hearts of the Body of Christ. Though He has revealed this of Himself from the very beginning, and never without a witness of it, history has never known a time frame marked by the entire Body of Christ living with Jesus' identity as Bridegroom being central and dominant. Yet the story of this age as revealed in the Word of God ends with the entire Church's surging return to her identity as the Bride of Christ and an erupting ascription to our betrothal to Him as our Bridegroom.

Before His return, the Body of Christ will know Him as Bridegroom and identify themselves corporately as His Bride, longing and crying out for His soon coming (Revelation 22:17). She will walk through the most difficult hour of her history in the most glorious display of identity—she will know who she is as His inheritance, His Bride.

The finale of this age is a great *wedding* as the pure and spotless Bride, the Church, is prepared and made ready for the wedding supper of the Lamb. With a joy and exultation that has been pent up in long anticipation-filled waiting and groaning for all the ages, finally, with one voice, we will come to the great summation of the ages. The great multitude, with a voice as the sound of many waters and mighty thundering, will cry out in glorious proclamation:

> Alleluia! For the Lord God Omnipotent reigns! Let us be glad and rejoice and give Him glory, for the marriage of the Lamb has come, and His wife has made herself ready. . . . "Blessed are those who are called to the marriage supper of the Lamb!"
>
> Revelation 19:6–9

We will love Him with every fiber of our being—all our heart, all our soul, all our mind and all our strength. We will agree with all that He is and all His ways, and find Him absolutely worthy and beautiful. The Father will behold a spotless Bride, made ready and prepared for His worthy Son, and the Son will receive His glorious inheritance, "holy and without blemish" (Ephesians 5:27).

It is with the full weight of this future and the full heart of this Holy Husband that Jesus' appeal to return to first love comes—a call increasingly poignant as this present age comes to a close. Jesus beckons His Church, individually and corporately. He calls as a bridegroom, with the heart and message He has always faithfully conveyed: He wants love at the center, and He refuses that love to grow cold (Matthew 22:37; 24:12).

The Penetrating Power of the Bridegroom's Heart

I stood alone in the sparsely green yard behind my duplex—a makeshift home for me and a handful of my Bible school friends—on that spring night at age 21, looking up at the night sky and the stars that He hung and knew by name. I was in transition, and I knew it; but the transition was interior and had to do with my beliefs about the heart of Jesus. An old mindset was being deconstructed piece by piece, and it felt as though I'd been in a wrestling match and was coming to the end of my strength. On one side of the match was my view of a God who was mostly disappointed with me, continually viewing me as coming up short, and on the other side was a God who was filled with delight and joy, jealously desiring and committed to bringing me into the fullness of His love and purpose. That night was a culmination of many months of hearing truths about Jesus' heart, emotions and nature that felt altogether new to my understanding. And something in me gave way. I quit fighting Him. It was as though the unrelenting waters finally broke through the dam of my soul and I submitted my arguments and resistance to the grace that had before seemed too good to be true.

I once heard John Piper use the phrase "grace at the gut level," and I thought, *That's what happened to me.*[3] I can think of no greater language to capture what I experienced when the light of Jesus' identity as the Bridegroom broke into my understanding. The truth that though my love was weak and still immature, He delighted in it and received it as real, authentic and beautiful. The truth that though I was dark, He called me lovely, broke into my 21-year-old heart like waves (Song of Songs 1:5). His grace billowed over me with His resolved jealousy and undeserved delight. This broke through to the most vulnerable and guarded parts of me. And this is what we need to restore first love: *grace to the gut.*

When passion cools somewhere along the way, we forget, and He wants to remind us again. The degree of our passion for Jesus is directly tied to whatever measure we have encountered and experienced of His passion for us.

As the Bridegroom, He appeals to our hearts. There's nothing like knowing Jesus as the Bridegroom. Nothing surpasses the encounter of getting near to the matchless splendor of who He is in this part of His identity. No part of His person is neutral, and every revelation of His nature transforms the human heart by transcendent potency.

> **No part of His person is neutral, and every revelation of His nature transforms the human heart by transcendent potency.**

In the Word, the Lord reveals Himself in many ways. He's the trusted Master, the worthy and honorable King, the loving Savior and the tender Shepherd. He is our Brother, our Lord and our Redeemer. Every aspect of who He is proves His holy transcendence and worth above any other person in heaven and on earth. Yet He is also the *holy Husband*—the divine Bridegroom, who has loved us with an everlasting love, and no other identity conveys His heart so vividly. No other part of Him pierces the receiving heart so directly and so deeply.

As the Bridegroom, His joy and passion rush to center stage as His unmerited kindness and unabashed tenderness grab hold of our hearts, turning them inside out again and again. The *loyalty* He demonstrates as Husband will reduce us to tears, and the desire He reveals will incite a holy trembling in our souls. His unrelenting affection and gentleness so rich will scatter the fog of our fears and shatter the weight of our shame. It's tenacious love we find here. It's who He is, and it undoes the human soul.

He is not just *like* a bridegroom. He *is* a bridegroom! In the truest sense of the identity, He is Jesus the Bridegroom. But what does this *mean*? What does this reveal of Him? Or of us?

The understanding of Jesus as Bridegroom is primarily about the *passion of* His heart and the *proximity to* that heart in covenantal love that He has brought us into. Our relationship to the Lord as the Bridegroom speaks of the closest relationship possible—the relationship of the marriage covenant. There is no *higher relationship* than the espousal relationship and no *stronger bond* than the bond of marriage. It conveys that we have been brought as near as we could have possibly been. And as we are brought so unfathomably near, we find the deepest love and the richest emotions.

Not only will we experience His affections and passion, but we will encounter His burning jealousy that preserves and keeps us. In those times when we fear we might lose our way, rather than deflating in discouragement, we will rise in confidence and assurance, resting in the truth that the One with the eyes like a flame of fire is the One whose gaze continually rests upon us. He is after each of us, and He is unrelenting. *He will not yield!*

Jesus does not cease to chase us down until He conquers our hearts—our all—completely. With each time He draws us, each way He hedges us in from pursuing other loves, it's as though He is saying, "I want it *all*. I want it *all*. Everything—heart, soul, mind and strength." This is the One who loves us. And, oh, the safety we find in knowing the jealousy that is in His heart for us.

You cannot touch this part of His identity and leave unchanged. It's meddling. It's invasive. It's the kind of thing that gets into that narrow space in the depths of your heart—the space that you guard and defend and protect. Here you are pierced, your guard brought low and your defenses set aside. Here He wins you to Himself.

Confidence in His kindness, His desire and His jealousy over us will take us places in love and obedience that no amount of willpower can muster. You might be able to deny a taskmaster. You might be able to ignore a distant god or a disappointed king. But when the One you serve is in your face with His tenacious, pursuing heart, He is hard to disregard or turn down. When I'm confident that He is *joyful* and full of *passion* and *desire* for me, and that though I am weak, He is kind, even tender with me in my weakness, I begin to *sprint* the course of love and obedience. My passion is but an overflow of His.

Love begets love. And when we come near to this potent and holy unfolding of His love and affections so powerful, our hearts—if willing—are left wounded by love, altered by His affection and utterly undone. Whether it is the first time we've beheld Him in His beauty as the Bridegroom, or we are coming back to be renewed in holy passion once more, this is the fuel. We love because He first loved, and love is both *awakened* and *reignited* in us directly according to the measure of the love of God we've known (1 John 3:16). Living in the confidence of this divine desire and jealousy causes our hearts to come alive *and to stay alive* in love and obedience.

Tender Affections Must Be Guarded

When He touches the most vulnerable parts of our hearts with His voice that says, "You are Mine," we enter the safety of confidence in love: the assurance of His affection. And here we must heed the proverb to guard our hearts at all costs (Proverbs 4:23). First love is that first receiving and believing in the love He has for us—extravagant and undeserved. Many foes oppose the tenderness and openheartedness here, and with one lie of the enemy or one nod to doubt, we can involuntarily throw up the distances that have us hiding and have the Lord asking,

"Where are you?" (Genesis 3:9). Guarding this secret exchange of our hearts with the Lord and His love is so necessary to keep enclosed the garden of our fellowship and friendship with Him (Song of Songs 4:12). As the words of the song beckon:

> I want your heart, and I want it all.
> Not just a part, but I want the whole.
> You know My voice, can you hear My call?
> I want your heart, and I want it all.
> I've given up everything, I've given you all of Me.
> Would you open your heart again,
> would you open your heart to Me?
>
> Remember when you first said yes?
> You gave it all and nothing less.
> Now years have come, and years have gone.
> But am I still your only One?
>
> I've given up everything, I've given you all of Me.
> Would you open your heart again,
> would you open your heart to Me?
> Just look at My nail-pierced hands,
> put yours in My wounded side.
> I'm asking for all your heart 'cause I've given you all of
>   Mine.[4]

As the Bridegroom, He calls us by name. And in His call, we hear an invitation to return so far beyond what we might have ever known in the past. In His voice are the grounding notes of Eden, when the Lord called to Adam in the cool of the day, "Where are you?" His call carries the drawing power of the Lamb slain, who gave Himself to us as the greater Hosea for us, His harlot Bride, Jew and Gentile.

"I'm calling you back to Myself. Like I called Adam in the Garden, I'm calling you by name. Return to Me." That which awakened us in the beginning has not diminished in its power to stir us again. He who called us at first now calls us again. And when our desire has dwindled, we must seek not to resuscitate it directly, but rather to return to the Source from which it was first born—to the *Person* who alone evokes thirsts old and new in us, every time we see, touch or taste of Him.

This sacred space, this glorious exchange in the depth of hearts—where we take His delight and love for us personally, guarding the warmth of our confidence in His cherishing love—this is where the battle is won or lost. Though we will fall short and though our deficiencies are real, we do not base our confidence in ourselves or in the strength of our own love, but in the everlasting affection of Christ Jesus. This is where we abide and draw our strength day by day and hour by hour. And when our own desire wanes, when we feel the frailty of our passion, the key is always returning to Him, to His unquenchable love and desire. When we do, He does something that He alone can do in us. He stirs our affections by reopening our thirsts and piercing our aching once again.

PRAYER

Jesus, I love You because You first loved me. I hear You calling me by name as the jealous Bridegroom, and my heart is moved at the sound of Your voice. Would You awaken my passion as I behold Yours? Would You strike my heart with revelation of Your jealous affection and zeal for me—causing my heart to burn? Would You tenderize my spirit with Your grace and gentleness toward me, even in my weakness, until I fully receive this love and acceptance in Your heart for me?

STEPS FORWARD IN KEEPING PASSION FOR JESUS

- To what degree have you known God's "grace to the gut," and have you drifted from it? Jesus' passion for *us* is the very fire that stirs and keeps our passion for Him. In order to take steps forward in keeping this flame, you must become a student of His affection for you, specifically in His identity as the Bridegroom. Go on an extended search through Scripture (or take note as you read the Word) to discover and meditate upon His emotions toward His people as the Bridegroom, and our identity before Him as the Bride . . . until His grace and affection undoes your heart at the deepest level.

- Each time you see this revelation in Scripture, ask the Holy Spirit to tenderize your heart through it, and in worshipful prayer, offer your affection back to Him.

Embracing the Ache of Holy, Vulnerable Desire for God

Maybe I had buried the pain that I had over the aches of early prayers yet unanswered. In the years of delay, I had gradually and imperceptibly decided God's answer was *no*. Delay and desire are not typically welcomed or anticipated companions. The vulnerability of unanswered hunger wears upon the heart. Without realizing it, we can back away from the expectation in order to cope with the pain of seeming rejection. Yet these conclusions are not grounded in the truth.

I remember pacing back and forth in my small living room in my early twenties, considering one question over and over in my heart and mind: *Why not me?*

For the previous few years, my spirit had been strikingly awakened by Jesus. Though I had loved Him sincerely as a child and into my youth, suddenly all that I'd ever known of Him before paled compared with the *splendid color* and beauty before me. He was a real man. He was alive and seated upon the throne, soon to return. He was the Bridegroom, who had a strong passion and desire for His people, and His desire was that we would know Him, truly know Him. His Word was living—a vast treasury to be searched out in pursuit of knowing and loving this Man Christ Jesus.

The wide-open invitation put forth in the Word of God to discover the inexhaustible pleasures of knowing Him compelled me like nothing ever had in my life. I remember biblical prayers so new to me that they felt foreign in my mouth—pouring out from my heart with the warmth of fresh faith and newborn desires for their fulfillment. One of these prayers was the cry of Paul: "to comprehend . . . the width and length and depth and height—to know the love of Christ which surpasses knowledge . . . that you may be filled with all the fullness of God" (Ephesians 3:18–19). What did that mean? What did that look like? Why *not* me? Why couldn't *my own heart* enter into this knowing of "the love of Christ which surpasses knowledge"? To be "filled with all the fullness of God"?

Adding to this biblical vision were shining examples of some of the men and women of Church history who went so shockingly deep in knowing and loving Jesus, awakening my heart to the potential of an abandoned life of prayer, communion and holy devotion to God. I read of saints from Church history—men and women such as Teresa of Ávila and Bernard of Clairvaux—those so pierced by the love of Christ that they lived as though burning from within, their lives a shining display of holy passion and full, sacrificial givenness to God.

With my faith stirred at the possibility and the surety of God's Word, as well as provoked by those burning ones in history who had laid hold of the deep things of Jesus' heart, my heart erupted with the desirous response to God: *Why not me? Why can't I touch You as Your Word describes? Why can't I also know You to the measure they did? How tender can a heart be in loving You? How alive? How burning?*

It was the same in my thirties, though circumstances were different. Now it was while bouncing a baby or feeding a toddler that this aching persisted. Longings and groanings ascending to God in bite-sized prayers amid monotonous tasks. He'd wounded me with a vision of fullness that I could not shake— and didn't want to. I wanted all that He had for the human heart in intimacy with Jesus. I wanted to know the deep things of God and the beauty of Jesus, all that the Father would reveal about His Son, until my heart burned with the fullness of His love, until I could stand beside the apostle Paul, knowing I had fully entered into the prayer that he prayed for the experiential knowing and comprehending of the love of God in Christ Jesus (John 17:26; Ephesians 3:16–19).

What I didn't anticipate is that when the Lord awakens holy desires for Himself in His people, He begins something that often carries years of unfolding in its wake. He most often leads the human heart forward, not by quick fulfilments, but rather by years of cultivating that hunger and thirst—of *becoming* the burning prayers we pray (Psalm 109:4). And these delays are part of His affirmative answer to us.

A careful attention to God's character, as revealed in His Word, confronts the idea that He would deny a hungry heart. Delay the answer, *yes*. Prepare us for the answer through testing and refining, *yes*. But God-awakened hunger is always pointing far beyond itself, past the delays that follow and the fires that come behind it. In fact, the delays and the preparatory refining are all *part* of God's answer to our prayers, forerunning the fullness of the answer He intends to satisfy us with.

Did we think we could pray grand prayers, heaving with holy request, and then not go through the necessary preparation for the Lord to answer them? He delights to fill the hungry "with good things" (Psalm 103:5). He rewards "those who diligently seek Him" (Hebrews 11:6). He blesses those "who hunger and thirst for righteousness" (Matthew 5:6). He gives the desires of the heart to the one who delights herself in Him (Psalm 37:4). The one who sows to the Spirit reaps everlasting life (Galatians

6:8). God cannot be mocked (Galatians 6:7). He is the God who hears and answers. He avenges those who cry out to Him day and night, "though He bears long with them" (Luke 18:7).

Delays do not indicate His *refusal* but His *approval* of our hungry prayers. Fires of testing are not a punch in the face after we've waited in the wilderness of hunger; they are the burning flame that removes the dross—in order that the gold we have asked for might be bought from Him.

The fire and delay can strike us as *His denial* of our prayers, when we don't yet fully comprehend the holy origins of our hunger—carved in us by God's own hand—and when we don't yet see how jealous He is to answer them. The God who calls Himself an all-consuming fire is not passive but rather active about our love for Him. He refuses to leave it in a weak state; He desires to bring it forth in splendor. Again, the fire and the testing are not His denial of our desire for Him, but signs of His commitment and beginnings of His answer to our prayers to know Him.

When the Lord calls us back to first love, He first untangles and separates our wrong conclusions—assumptions that He is not going to answer our heart cries—from our precious hunger and desire for Him. Where we backed away and stifled the ache because of the disappointment of delay, He draws near to help us see where we believed wrong things about Him. He removes the sting of rejection that pricked us spirit, soul and body when we thought He was denying us. And then He asks us if we would willingly take up the thirst once more. He asks if we still desire from Him what we first desired.

When I became alerted to the fact that something was wrong at the heart level, I didn't know what the cause was. I didn't know why things had progressively begun to shut down or what had set in motion a slow dimming of yesterday's passion. Yet I knew He alone could give the answers. It was a winter I will never forget as I spent hours in front of my fireplace, day after day, stoking embers to fight off the cold—an ironic metaphor that was almost a prophetic picture of my own heart and its need for rekindling. And as I lifted to the Lord what felt like *a heart gone lifeless*, I was surprised at where He started. The first thing the Lord did as I came before Him, and as I waited upon Him in prayer and meditation upon His Word, was to fan the flame of those first desires by awakening them in me again and showing me where I'd misunderstood His response to them. I'd accepted delay as denial, but all along He had already begun His answer by sending the fire. When we have made the Lord our delight, He gives us the desires of our hearts—even if that giving begins with the refining of delayed answers.

Desire for Jesus

In my early years, when the Lord awakened my heart to see His beauty and affection like never before, I experienced a simultaneous awakening of hunger for Him—stronger than I'd ever known. Seeing more of His beauty caused both a deeper satisfaction and an increased thirsting for *more* of Him in my soul. *What would He give to the human heart if He had His full way with it? How far would He let me go in knowing Him if He found no reservation or doubt, but only a welcoming, faith-filled hunger and agreement in me? How deeply would He satisfy that cultivated desire?*

With fervent passion, I began to believe and cry out to God for the full measure He would give the human heart in this age, by His grace. Like a vast ocean of holy invitation opening before me into the depths of His heart and the fullness of joy in knowing Him, an insatiable aching arose in me to comprehend—together with all the saints—the fullness of His love (Ephesians 3:19). I began to cry out to see the full measure of His beauty and to experience the deepest fellowship with Him—as the Word of God describes.

Holy awakenings are the beginnings of new desires. What we were asleep to before, now we are brought to our senses to behold and cry out for. This is part of the Lord's leadership in our lives. He awakens holy desires that are knit to fresh faith in Him and in what His Word proclaims. These desires are not neutral. They alter the course of our lives and change our trajectories because they get to the bottom of our affections. Yet what is in Jesus' heart when He awakens these longings in us? When delays come and testings loom, does it mean His answer to these initial awakenings is *no*? Does it mean we believed in vain or believed for too much of God's grace? Or does it mean—as the Lord shifted my perspective to see—tests and delays are not His changing His mind, but testaments of His commitment to see those desires through to their fulfillment?

At the beginning, when the Lord Jesus awakens our hearts to His love, there is a simultaneous stirring of a deep desire and longing for Him. It's born of the Holy Spirit within our hearts. Love and longing are so closely tied that the minute you divide them, you've lost the essence of both. Love is not *love* without desire arising from it, and desire is not *desire* except that it proceeds from love. Thus, *to love Jesus is to long for Him.*

From our mother's womb, we are all created with a deep thirst. He put eternity in the heart of man, and we were made for God (Ecclesiastes 3:11). Yet this inherent capacity for God is different from the desires we experience after coming into the saving knowledge of Christ, having our affections awakened by His Spirit and tasting of His goodness and love. Here, our thirst for Him is more than an innate capacity for God; it is a yearning that carries *knowing* in its wings, a thirst not of *vacancy* but of *intimacy*. Peter described it as a desiring that comes out of the tasting of His goodness (1 Peter 2:2–3).

For all who know the Lord, desire for Him is the fruit of tasting. Hunger is the fruit of feasting. We love because He first loved us, and we desire because we've already known and experienced Jesus—His beauty, His kindness and His desire for us. C. S. Lewis termed this "inconsolable longing" for God *joy*, because though there is a "stabbing" of longing in it, anyone who has tasted it would never exchange it, not even for all the pleasures in the world.[1] It is not an aching out of emptiness, but out of *substance*.

First love for Jesus begins when the God-given tasting of His beauty and worth awakens a holy desire in us that refuses to be comforted except with that which we first tasted in Him. Thus, first love could also be called *first desire*, because every tasting awakens a greater longing for more of Him, and our hearts were awakened not only by tasting but also by new holy longings born of the Spirit of God. By His Spirit, we groan and ache for more of Him, until our aching is met with fullness (Romans 8:26–27).

> **First love for Jesus begins when the God-given tasting of His beauty and worth awakens a holy desire in us that refuses to be comforted except with that which we first tasted in Him.**

Longing for Jesus is unlike any other longing in that even the aching holds a sense of the experience of Jesus' beauty and love because He is unlike any other. As Peter described, those who have tasted of His goodness are altered forever (1 Peter 2:3). We don't return to what we were before we tasted of Him. Rather, with every taste, with every sight of Him, with every encounter of His love, experience of His grace and piercing by His words, we are both satisfied and left yearning for more. The desire is not only a wanting but a tasting of the sweetness we have known in Him. Like a hook in the heart, it fastens us to Him irrevocably. And when He desires to draw us after Himself, this is the ache that He pulls upon. He goes back to that first thirst and stirs it, causing us to pant after Him again.

When Jesus asks us to return to our first love, He is calling us to return to our first longing and desire for Him—to induce that thirst again. He reminds us that the deep aching we had for Him in the beginning was not of our own making but His hand upon us. He has not changed in His purpose and desire to answer and fulfill the longing He has marked us with. He calls our name and draws our heart by that early longing, beckoning us back to those tender affections for Him.

Longing and desire are the painful parts of love. They are the sides of love that hurt in delay, that ache and refuse to forget the "more" that Jesus has for us, unsatisfied with anything less. Our longing for Jesus always proclaims, "What I have is not enough," giving testimony to both how we have found Him to be the Source of all satisfaction, and how we have not fully been answered and won't be until the glorious future day when our faith in Jesus is finally made sight and our hope is fully realized. To love Him in this way is not always comfortable, but to love Him in a way devoid of aching is not love.

Longing for Jesus is sweet and welcomed by us in the beginning, yet often much more difficult as the years go by and we experience setbacks in our lives. When delay sets in and confusion knocks on the door, we are prone to wall up our hearts from the vulnerability of desire. We are professional self-protectors, and to stay in the place of aching is utterly crosscurrent to our common propensities. Yet loving Jesus cannot be devoid of longing for Him, and though there be a sting in the aching, He wants us to *return* to it as part of our love for Him.

Thus, when the Lord desires to draw us back to first love, He awakens the longings for Himself that He did at first. He draws us according to those initial achings—those first hooks in the heart. The desires for Jesus that shaped our paths at first are not incidental nor a onetime reality, and we do well to pay attention to them. Awakened by His hand, they are strategic and serve as promises of where we are headed and living testaments of what every part of the journey is aimed at.

Holy, Ageless Desire

Jesus surprises me in the way He leads. I look at my heart and feel discouraged because I don't know how to make it yearn as it did at first. I don't know how to reawaken my own affections. Yet this is no obstacle for Him. He is not limited by the rise and fall of my fervency because He Himself never wanes in fervency. He never grows weary in His desire nor fainthearted in His passion. Though the unfolding years and circumstances have taken their toll on me, though I have grown weary under the weight of difficulties, my own insufficiencies and disappointments, *He has not.* He has known no such depletion or burdening, and His passion and desire that awakened my heart at first have not changed even in the slightest degree.

And so, when we find our passion weary and sidelined, willing but unsure if it can be stirred again, He comes to us and does what He delights to do. He leans down to the flickering flame, the dimly burning wick, and He stirs the fire by rekindling the first desires for Himself (Isaiah 42:3). He renews us by inciting our deepest thirst—that vulnerable longing of love for Jesus that first stirred in us. And as He stimulates our hunger, we're rushed back to a place that we didn't think possible, tenderized by our initial longings for Him. Suddenly, a familiar yearning lays hold of us as though we'd never left it behind, and the weariness falls to the ground.

This reopening of the early desires showed me how much nearer He was in the aching than I had realized. I found myself suddenly surprised by the same yearning that I'd known at the very beginning—so many years ago. Like being rushed back in time, back to my youth, the hunger was the same. Bewildered by a desire that felt young, now in a life that had weathered some decades, it struck me: The desire was always *Him in me*. The desire was not subject to my aging, or the weariness of the years, because it was not born of *me*. It always was God within me—the One who never wearies, never changes, never grows old.

His presence was closer than I'd perceived in the very yearnings for more of Him. And this is because the Spirit of God within us, who glorifies and reveals Jesus to us, does not only pour out the love of God into our hearts, but groans and yearns within us, causing us to long for the One our souls love. His nearness and presence are found not only in the satisfactions but in the groanings—both experiences of love. To stifle our yearning for Him when the delays come, concluding that we were wrong to want so much of Him, is to suppress the activity of His Spirit within us. When He revived the longing again, I experienced the surprise that a renewed thirst was also a renewed sense of His presence. To return to desire for Jesus is to return to and find *Him*, for His nearness is there in the longing.

Discovering this leadership of Jesus in my own heart and life—this way He renews first love and passion by fueling the early longings again—caused my heart to cry out to Him in prayer:

How do tears of desire open decades in their wake? How do You tear me open to the place that doesn't age—in an instant taken back to a tenderness that never waned? How have years not aged this ache?

Perhaps there's a story in the hunger that remains young, and the tenderness that stays ageless while years march on. Perhaps this meeting place of my longing for You and Your coming to me cuts me open—and leaves me vulnerable—not to desires of my own making, but to a love and desire that are, in fact, You Yourself in me.

You, the One who never wearies. You, the ageless and unfainting One. It was always You in me. It was Your desire that stirred. Bodies age and hearts dull, but the longing of Jesus is eternal youth (Psalm 110:3). Your love is a most vehement flame—it never wanes. It can cut a heart open to first love and first desire in a moment, as though not a day had passed in between.

I've yet to find You fully, but the wanting is part of the truth. The desire that will burn in me is not Your hiding, but my finding of the everlasting flame that will warm the way. And when my heart opens up in love for You, I know that You have found me and will never let me go in that ache.

Our achings carry seeds of knowing—seeds of life that never die. We will never stand in the age to come and say, "You opened that longing, and You never answered." Rather, of every hunger we carried and every yearning that we embraced, we will say, "You were in the hunger, and You were in the satisfying. Every aching for Yourself that You opened up in me, You filled abundantly."

Reopening the Ache

The heart that possesses expectant longing is prone toward sickness amidst delay, just as the wisdom of Proverbs 13:12 warns: "Hope deferred makes the heart sick, but a longing fulfilled is a tree of life" (NIV). Openhearted, hopeful longing is difficult to steward over decades. When hope opens the heart with desire but then waits in unanswered delay, sickness will inevitably creep in, uninvited. And yet this proverb reaches beyond a warning and opens up into a promise: *A longing fulfilled is a tree of life.*

Hope in God does not have to end in sickness of heart, and desire does not have to bend toward disillusionment. Though longing for anything of this world will surely sicken the heart when it ends in futility, the desire for Jesus—born of the Holy Spirit—leads us to invincible satisfaction. God's purpose for the work of desire for Himself is the opposite of shriveling in sickness; it is to be met with foretastes of the Tree of Life until this age is over, and faith is made sight, hope is realized and at last every longing is fulfilled in Him.

Jesus is a better leader than we are followers. He is the great Physician, and we are those in need of healing. He knows how to resuscitate our panting for Him, to wash away the erosion of sickness and to cause our hearts to burn with hopeful yearning once more. We grow sick when what began as hope gives way to despair. The delay speaks louder to our souls than the promise, and accusations lurk with arguments and condemnations more compelling than ever. Yet Jesus sees right through the snare of these adversaries and calls us back to the hope we had at first.

Have we changed? Yes.

Have the circumstances weighed us down and the delay sickened our hearts? Yes.

But does that mean hopeful longing cannot endure the distance? No. Because hopeful longing is born of God, not of ourselves. It is not a self-conjured ache, but a God-breathed yearning that possesses within it a true tasting of Christ, the Satisfier.

When the Spirit of God renews us by washing away the weariness and stirring the fires of desire, we are not brought back to ourselves *but to Him*. We do not return to a lost part of our hearts, *but to His holy heart* that has no shadow of turning and no diminishing of burning (James 1:17). Yes, it is an aching that we take part in and voluntarily receive, but it is, nonetheless, holy and born not of our own souls, but of Him. It is a seed waiting to be a tree—a holy yearning with an indestructible, living hope beneath it (1 Peter 1:3–4).

Desire Fulfilled: A Tree of Life

First love is intricately knit to awakened longings for Jesus—when the treasure is found, and the vows are made, or when the taste is experienced and longing for fullness reaches out from the deepest heart (Matthew 13:44; 1 Peter 2:3). The true knowledge of Jesus, the tasting of His goodness, is not neutral in its effects upon our souls. It is a tasting that utterly transforms our appetites to long for Him alone. Yet we are prone to doubt, to believe accusations, to grow weary in waiting and to give in to unbelief. Jesus is saying that to return to first love is to come back to desires you drew back from, you stifled and abandoned—for the sickness of heart they were causing. Those longings were not wrong, though they were met with testing and delay. They were not romanticized overreaching, but *rightful* expectancy.

Yet first love and the keeping of it is a war, with adversaries that must be overcome. Sickness is the bent of the human heart awakened in love and hope, but then tested by trials, accusations and delay. This is what Jesus invites us to overcome. When love is lost because of sickness of heart, because of a crushed spirit, we need Him to come and shine His light upon the causes. Was it the accusations? Was it His seeming silence? Was it the circumstances that weighed heavier than our hope? Was it the division of our affection over time? Where did the lies seep in and the accusations take root? What got into the garden of our souls and stole the vibrancy of our sincere desire for God?

A longing for Jesus kept and a heart continued in sincere and hopeful yearning for Him—open and unoffended—will be rewarded by Him forever. He blesses those who hunger and thirst for righteousness and promises that they will be filled

(Matthew 5:6). This precious longing for Him is a gift that He gives to us by His grace and then rewards us for keeping and fighting to preserve it in our hearts and lives.

Jesus' promise to the one who overcomes, the one who resists the temptation to lose his first love and fights to return to it and keep it alive, is that He will grant him to eat of the Tree of Life, which is in the paradise of God (Proverbs 13:12; Revelation 2:7). This wisdom from Proverbs compels us not to give in to the sickness that openhearted longing can lead to when that desire is deferred, for it points us to the promise of the Tree of Life found at the end of this age (Proverbs 13:12; Revelation 22:2). He gives us foretastes now of the coming day when our precious, holy longing will at last be fully satisfied—when Christ Himself will call us overcomers and reward us by granting us to eat from the Tree of Life, the tree whose leaves will heal the nations and whose fruit will only be given to those who have washed their robes and been given the right to it (Revelation 22:2, 14).

It's hard to say exactly how the Lord did it, but as I sought Him in prayer, asking Him to restore and renew me from any dimming of love, He first put His hand upon my desires, restoring them, and I began to hunger for the things I had hungered for at first, not with an aged and diminished yearning, but one fervent and strong, just like at first. Those early longings I had carried—for the full measure that He would give the human heart, that my eyes would behold His beauty and my heart would be filled with His love—came out of what felt like a slumber to a full thirst again (Ephesians 1:17–19, 3:16–19). And as these desires were reawakened, something took me by surprise: I felt *inwardly renewed*, as though no years had transpired from my youth. He is the One who satisfies our desires with good things so that our youth can be renewed like the eagle's, so that our youth keeps coming back (Psalm 103:5). These words of David seem to express exactly what I experienced in those days. He awakened the early desires and satisfied me with the assurance of *hope* in His answer and renewing my youth like the eagle's.

When the Lord reopened the ache in me that cut back the years in a moment, I scribbled words through tears, filling journal pages that once stared back at me blankly, now receiving a pent-up flood of fresh hope, washing over the heartache. I wrote:

> The paths are less beaten down, but familiar as friendship, the places I waited for You. And You were quiet, and I was quick to doubt. And the vulnerability made the waiting even more pronounced. Is it me? Is it You? Where does rejection, so ready, lay its blame? Why, when I called, did You not answer? Why, when I waited, did You not come? The wrestlings of my youth faded slowly into the back seat of life's middle of the road. Now there was more to life than these deep desires. Small bodies to hold, hearts to lead, places to be. And I put a little distance between that meeting ground of rawest longing and Your wanting of me.
>
> The little bodies grew. The hearts entered wrestlings of their own. And I tried to lead through love and truth that I'm still fighting so hard to hold.
>
> Maybe You're beckoning me back to conversations we never finished, to waitings I was never to leave, to desires meant to stay raw. Maybe desires aren't to stay in our youth but to lead us and our children all the way home. Maybe You're bringing me all the way back to familiar wrestlings and beaten paths because the dream was not a dream I made up but a promise as sure as the dawn.

Keeping Desire for Jesus Alive and Pure

Our desire for Jesus is essential, and this is why the Lord revives it when we have drawn back from it. In all of my doings, all of my comings and goings, all of my seasons and all of life's twists and turns, I want my desire for Jesus to be as a fiery flame, unquenched and strong. Where desire has grown dull is where I have lost the very heart of life. Where hunger for Him has been pacified is where I have settled for distractions rather than highest delight.

Desire for Jesus is so precious. The more desirous we are for the Lord, the more truly alive we are. Conversely, the degree of our lack of hunger is the degree of our deadness and the measure of our disconnect from what we were fashioned for. *We were made for Him.*

Our hunger, not fearing delays or the pain of yearning, hears all that is available, all that the future holds in fullness, all that the Creator intended for the present, and it reaches beyond itself until that fullness is found, until that perfect day dawns. Desire escorts us to the desirable One and helps us refuse to be comforted by anything or anyone less.

Most of the time, our problem is not that we want Him too much but that we want Him too little. As C. S. Lewis said so insightfully,

> If we consider the unblushing promises of reward and the staggering nature of the rewards promised in the Gospels, it would seem that Our Lord finds our desires not too strong, but too weak. We are half-hearted creatures, fooling about with drink and sex and ambition when infinite joy is offered us, like an ignorant child who wants to go on making mud pies in a slum because he cannot imagine what is meant by the offer of a holiday at the sea. We are far too easily pleased.[2]

Though desperation may be looked down upon, and though some might say we are only to be content, we fool ourselves into thinking that shutting down desire is doing ourselves a favor. That wanting more of God is not our portion. Desire and delight are intricately knitted, and you cannot have one without the other. Thus, to neglect the thirst of desire or to shut it down in weariness is to simultaneously forfeit the joy of delight. We can only delight in as much as we have desired (Psalm 37:4).

So, our prayer must be that desire for Jesus would prevail over every area of passivity or indifference in our souls—that we would not be easily pleased with less than what He wants to give us in Him, but rather cry out for the full measure that is in His heart. May He awaken us into the dignity of wanting more of Him. May an aching desire for Him fill our minds, hearts and souls, and may He draw our affections out of distraction and dullness and sickness of heart and awaken us to the precious and holy longing for which we were fashioned.

A. W. Tozer said, "Complacency is a deadly foe of all spiritual growth. Acute desire must be present or there will be no manifestation of Christ to His people. He waits to be wanted. Too bad that with many of us He waits so long, so very long, in vain."[3]

Only the hungry get Jesus. Only the desperate find Him. Let us not keep the Lord waiting for our wanting of Him. Let us lift our hunger to Him and ask that He breathe on it, that He cause it to increase. Let us recount every taste that we have had of His goodness and of the glories to come, that our souls might be lifted from the slum of dullness and distraction and disillusionment and return to the sheer pleasure of holy passion for Him (Psalm 34:8; Hebrews 6:5).

> **Only the hungry get Jesus. Only the desperate find Him.**

Part of the way we keep our thirst for Jesus is keeping Him as our only Source. We are to keep coming back to Him as our Fountain, the Fountain that only the thirsty are invited to drink from. When the Lord spoke to Israel of forsaking Him as the Fountain, He exposed the bent of every human heart to hewn broken cisterns as an escape route (Jeremiah 2:13). We fear not being answered and thus multiply our options. Yet the Lord is jealous over the entirety of our thirst. We cannot multitask our hunger or divvy out our thirst to multiple sources. A divided thirst—to the Lord—is not a thirst, even as friendship with the world is no longer friendship with God (James 4:4). Singular thirsting is what He's after when He says, "Let him who thirsts come" (Isaiah 55:1; John 7:37; Revelation 22:17).

He wants to unify our thirsts until we long for Him alone. So often, we come to the Fountain, and though we truly want a drink, we do not realize the multiplicity of our souls. If we could see as He sees, we would perceive the partiality in our thirsting. We come with sincerity, but it's only a sliver of the soul. We truly thirst for Him, yet we have so many backup plans—so many hewn cisterns right behind us. Though broken and without water, they still occupy our capacity for thirst, for we wouldn't have hewn them for ourselves if we did not somewhat believe they'd quench us.

Being empty isn't what derails us, but being partially satisfied is. Our desperation deceives us when it is a divided cry with secondary options. He is anything but an option among many. When He said, "All you who are thirsty," or "If anyone thirsts," or "Let him who thirsts come," He did not call the one with divided desire or the one who has a wanting with a Plan B in case it doesn't work out. No, to the contrary, He called the one who has no other options, no other cisterns from which to draw, no other fountains from which to drink.

My own experience had been a bursting forth of youthful desire, fervent and innocent and right. The years that followed, filled with the usual elements that life brings, not only threatened these fervent desires with the disillusionment that can set in with all of life's circumstantial twists and turns, but with a gradual and even imperceptible second-guessing of that for which I had originally believed God. *Maybe I had asked and believed for too much. Maybe I had misunderstood what the*

74

Lord desired to give to the human heart in friendship and communion with Him.

These were subtle and well-beneath-the-surface deductions that wouldn't even become exposed until, once again, He renewed and reopened these first desires. And I would then know how precious and holy such early hungers were. I would behold how Jesus is too jealous over us to leave hidden these false conclusions that hinder our love for Him. He refuses to allow even subtle unbelief to lurk within our love for Him. He is ever committed to finish the work that He started and to bring us forth in full love, with full and fervent desire for Him, to the end (Philippians 1:6).

PRAYER

Jesus, You have awakened desire for Yourself in me and I receive it as one of the most precious gifts available to the human heart. Wherever my hunger has grown dull, I ask You to awaken it again. I commit to embracing the desires for You that fuel my love for You, not quenching them with the love of other things or through the sickness that can come by misinterpreted delays. I trust You. I love You. Let desire for You come to full fire in me again.

STEPS FORWARD IN KEEPING PASSION FOR JESUS

- First, ask Jesus for eyes to recognize your hunger and desire for Him as *gifts of God*, that you might embrace these yearnings by offering them up to Him with your voluntary love and affection.

75

- If your heart has grown sick with the pain of delay, bring this discouragement to Him in prayer. Allow Him to heal these areas in your heart as the light of His Word shines like a spotlight, dispelling dark conclusions of His rejection and igniting new faith in His commitment to answer your thirst for Him.

- Finally, to keep and guard over this most precious thirst for Him, tell Him of your commitment to keep Him as your only Source by asking the Holy Spirit to highlight to you anything apart from Him that is holding partial claim on your affections. Wherever the Lord reveals dividedness in your love through desires for other things, repent and turn your affection to Him alone, making tender statements of your loyalty to Him in prayer and asking for His grace to keep Him as your only Source.

Repenting of Unbelief and Recovering Confident Trust

would have told you I didn't suffer from unbelief. I never would have diagnosed limping passion for Jesus as struggling trust. And perhaps, had fervency not slowed, I would have never caught on to anything gone awry deep within. Yet this is often the sequence of slowed affection. It was for me.

My trust was under fire, and I hadn't realized it. Though I had a growing concern for dimmed vibrancy, I did not realize how you can often trace a line from fainting affection back to a quaking confidence. And Jesus did that for me.

I sat, as it were, on the side of the road, brokenhearted because my desire to love Him was so sincere. But sincerity does not possess resurrection power. And it was as though He came to me there, kneeling down and looking me in the eye.

"Jesus, You know that I love You," I said to Him.

And with a question asked for my sake, not for His, He responded: "Yes, but do you *believe* Me?"

Yes, of course I believe You, I was quick to assure.

No, you've quit fully believing something at the heart level, something so fundamental to loving Me: You've lost your confidence of My delight in you. It's there that you've quit believing Me. . . . His unanticipated evaluation came back to me.

My arguments with Him in this continued because I was slow to believe something so basic could be my story, but in time, of course, I found Him to be right.

Love does not cool without cause. Desire shuts down for a reason. Beneath dimmed longings for Jesus is the scaffolding we've built out of our false beliefs, conscious or unperceived. First love includes a present-tense sense of His affection, abiding in it and believing it—not just with mental assents that age, but with a childlike trust always young.

The barrage of accusations we undergo as believers with a real adversary is not neutral and can wear down our confidence over time, until our faith ultimately begins to break down. Or, the emotional aftermath of painful circumstances and disappointments can place a heavy toll on us, leading to offenses, fear, bitterness and cynicism—all deconstructors of what we first believed of Him—if not carefully walked out with the Lord.

These subtle belief systems we've erected become exposed when cooled love alerts us to their hiding. Affections gone lifeless make us go searching for the deeper sickness, and it's here that the Lord brings us to see the lurking culprit below: *unbelief.*

The Real Adversaries of the Heart

Our paths and circumstances all vary, but the results are often much the same. Whether our story is riddled with broken relationships, financial difficulties, sickness or prodigal children, *inward offense* is often the outcome.

God, where are You? God, why? We struggle to trust the Lord with our losses, our hearts weighed down with grief. *God, how could You allow this to happen?*

Disillusionment can set in when things don't play out as we had hoped or when our own failures slam us against the wall of disappointment. We draw back from the Lord inwardly. We reevaluate. *What am I doing with my life? Did I even hear the Lord?*

Cynicism knocks and can take over as things go on as they have for years on end. The rolling of the eyes sets in. *I've seen it all before. Here we go again.* Or, *Oh yeah, just give it time. You'll see.*

These offenses, in all their varying shades, are not neutral to love. It is in the wake and increase of such offenses that Jesus describes the love of many growing cold (Matthew 24:12). The battles that come and the enemies that war against our first love for Jesus are *many*, and they come in unique ways to each of us, but it seems their effects on the heart can often share a common cause. Underneath the offenses—below the sour fruit of bitterness, the weeds of disillusionment and the thorns of anger—is the twisting root system of unbelief. Unbelief is the opposite of faith, and love for Jesus cannot survive—and certainly cannot flourish—without a continual burning faith in Him.

This is where the heart sins imperceptibly and unwittingly. We can fight hard against offense, against bitterness, against culprits of love growing cold, and still lose heart because of the undercurrents of unbelief. We seldom realize until the aftermath that we're not the children of faith that we once were, that somewhere along the way we grew up and grew cold in our system of believing, that skepticism seeped in, eroding our love and affection.

Love grown cold is most often the culmination of fainting faith and hope deferred. Our confidence before God is knit to our beliefs about Him. If we begin to subtly believe He is not as good as we'd thought, because of the collisions of what He's allowed or not allowed in our lives, or if we begin to gradually believe the lurking accusations against His heart—that He is disappointed in us or that His heart is closed toward us—our confidence before Him deteriorates. We can never maintain openhearted trust toward the Lord unless we stand confident before His throne of grace. Resilient faith springs forth from possessing bold assurance before Him in love.

When buoyant confidence in the Lord gives way, love is gradually threatened in its wake. One swallow of lies and half-truths at a time, we accept the poison of accusation against the Lord and against our own hearts. We can major on love and minor on faith, but this catches up to us in the end, because the Lord is after "*faith working through love*" (Galatians 5:6). Love gets broken and sidelined without faith working its way through it, coursing through its veins. Faith and love are to work together in us, but if we give in to the chipping away of confidence in Jesus—that He is good and that He will do what He promised in His Word—in the end, we find a heart that no longer loves as it once did. The lie against His goodness and faithfulness to do what He has promised gets in like an arrow to the heart of everything. The greatest enemy of the first commandment is unbelief.

The real adversaries of the heart are not circumstances, but what the heart does with the Lord *beneath* the circumstances. All the difficulties and troubles can rail against the soul, while Paul can still come up in joy, declaring, "No, in all these things we are more than conquerors through him who loved us" (Romans 8:37 NIV). All the losses can add up and multiply, while John proclaims, "Let it decrease. I've heard the voice of the Bridegroom, and my joy is made full" (see John 3:29–30).

So the real enemies are not what happens to us, or what unfolds through life's circumstances, but the accusations and offenses that we allow to slither into the inner garden—just like that first snake of old. They are the subtle tastes and agreement with poisonous lies that corrupt the space in the holy exchange between our heart and the Lord's. The question deeper than

What was the offense? or *What was the circumstance that led to the cynicism?* is *When and why did you give in to doubt and unbelief about the love of Christ for you?*

What we do outwardly is directly tied to what we believe inwardly. And it's here in our inmost perspectives where the arrows fly, and the target is wide. The root of the tree is what we believe. And lest we fool ourselves into assuming we believe something we don't, we must ask Him to search and know our hearts; mental assents are deceptive stand-ins for core beliefs. And though our outward actions give us insights, God alone can diagnose the deepest places and enlighten our darkness.

We must see the Lord's kind and zealous leadership over our hearts and lives. We, like Peter, are heartsick over our love's failure, yet Jesus sees these crises as the very way forward into love made holy and mature. He uncovers our unbelief, not to expose us as frauds or hypocrites, but out of His joyful zeal, He does this to transform our authentic love for Him into proven and tested love, refined as gold. Out of Peter's failed devotion, He brought forth the one He called *the rock.* And part of the process of keeping first love all our days is His leading us through the paths that finally expose the hidden unbelief that threatens our love for Him.

Oh, the amount of patience it takes to lead as Jesus leads! He leads us in such a way that voluntary love is preserved at every step, all the way to the end. He kneels down in front of us, tenderly speaking truth and love to our hearts and shining His light on ensnaring areas of unbelief. Roadblocks to us are never hindrances to Him. All resurrection power belongs to Him. But He wants us to choose, to partner, to believe and to walk forward with Him voluntarily. He'll take a lifetime of highs and lows, twists and turns, to carefully bring forth victorious love in us—without the shadows of fear and unbelief.

Returning to Childlike Trust

Though unbelief seeks to hide and mask and maneuver, one of the places it lurks most menacingly is in our interior confidence and belief in Jesus' pleasure over us. We subtly start swallowing accusations against the truth of His love—from the enemy, from others and from our own hearts—and the result is a gradual loss of confidence before Him.

If the accusations of the enemy were loud and bold, said directly to our faces, we might be more apt to reject them. Yet since that first conversation with the snake in the Garden, accusations toward God have a way of slithering in unperceived in their subtlety. These cunning charges against the Lord and against our own hearts become an atmosphere of accusation in our hearts and minds. We begin to live under a persistent residue of accusation and condemnation, and a subsequent weakening of openhearted trust in our souls, ultimately rendering us sidelined.

Such loss of assurance in this most vulnerable place can't help but bear the fruit of anxiety, and sometimes it's our anxiety that first alerts us that we have, in fact, drifted from our first love. Anxiety is the opposite of confidence, and it serves as an exposer of our lost sense of Jesus' affection and delight in us. We may be going through all the outward motions and convincing ourselves that our hearts are fine. Yet imperceptibly and without warning, anxiety builds as our subtle unbelief in His love for us sets in. This low-grade anxiety tells the story of a heart that somewhere along the way quit fully believing in His love for us, in His ever-present, unconditional, heart-open affection for us. With that loss of confidence comes the burden of performance, the disquieting of fear and the angst of joy lost.

Jesus said the root of anxiety is lack of faith in our heavenly Father (Matthew 6:25–34). As unbelief gets the upper hand in our hearts, one of the results is this angst within. Somewhere along the way, we aged out of the wonder, of the openhearted confidence and trust. When we're anxious, our trust has shifted out of childlike, awe-filled faith in Him—the trust we had at first.

What is it about the human heart that believes growing in maturity means leaving behind childlikeness, abandoning simple trust? Sometimes it takes a lifetime in Christ for us to finally become children. And the childlike trust that we possessed at first is often the first to go as the years pass, as we experience setbacks and become more burdened with cares, disillusioned with circumstances and wounded by the arrows that fly.

The Lord calls us back to the simplicity of believing, to the ease of trust in Him that we first had. First love is that first believing and receiving of the love He has for us. We believed without hesitation and received His love without boundaries. With childlike trust, we took Him at His Word as the Good News of the Gospel laid hold of us. We knew that His love was the great glory of our lives, and our weakness and deficiencies were no contenders for that force.

Abiding in His love, believing that He rejoices over me—this is where anxieties and fears weaken and dissolve in their hold, and my heart is set free. A softening of heart comes through believing that He tenderly receives me. This is one of the defining qualities of *first love*—strong at first, yet so easy to lose over time. The moment we step away from the shadow of the cross—where we first met His undeserved love and were washed and utterly undone by a love that offers itself freely and based on nothing we have done or will do—we begin to lose the heart of everything, one inch at a time. Every step we take away from under that blessed shadow, we subtly revert to old patterns of performance and to experience the anxiety that accompanies them.

Years of unfolding circumstances and hope deferred often bring what Chesterton admitted: "We have sinned and grown

83

old, and our Father is younger than we."[1] With the years comes the weight of our weakness, the war against dullness and the enemies of doubt and unbelief. And we can slowly lose the continual, gut-level believing that He delights in us—in you and in me. We shift subtly away from His opinion and gradually give in to our own, or to the accusations poised to be received. Slowly over time, there comes the erosion of that first trust that leapt out into wholehearted love without a second thought.

The voice of the accuser grows louder throughout the compounding seasons of life. Every voice—the enemy's, the world's and even our own—comes in like the serpent of old to strangle the simplicity of devotion to Christ (2 Corinthians 11:3). The disapproving voices of others around us can multiply and drown out the truth. And in these times, unless we contend in the opposite direction of those accusations, we can form ever-so-subtle assumptions that Jesus also feels this way about us. We subconsciously lump His perspective in with the voices of accusation that hover, and instead of holding fast to the truth of His Word and His love, we draw back.

> **Slowly over time, there comes the erosion of that first trust that leapt out into wholehearted love without a second thought.**

The enemy aims his weapon straight at the heart. If he can make his mark straight into that space of confidence, he has won. The greatest warfare of first love is believing God's Word and His love for us. When that confidence is gone, we're just going through the motions, hurting and giving up the dream. An arrow at the heart of it all—the secret place of confidence—is all it takes. Accusation, unchecked and granted entrance, sickens the roots of the tree, our core beliefs, and eventually bears the fruit of unbelief.

Returning to first love is not so unlike returning to the first days. The outward actions that we did initially came from the inward movements of what we believed at first—and the simplicity of that trust. I believed that He loved me, that He forgave me fully and accepted me completely. I took up the cup of salvation with a ready heart and received, just received (Psalm 116:12). To go back, then, is to lay aside our doubt and distrust, reaching in faith and confidence to believe.

Jesus does not want this precious flame of faith to be lost. Where confidence is lost, unbelief—that thief of love—seeks to creep in. It can land a lover of God on the side of the road, derailed and disillusioned. If not dealt with by repentance, and then by restoration of the Healer, the loss can be fatal. Even love can be lost in unbelief's wake. There's nothing heavier to carry than a cold heart, weighed down with unbelief. Jesus calls us back to the tenderness, back to the childlike believing, back to delight and wonder. All is still true. *Simplicity of devotion is simplicity of trust and believing.* It is throwing out the serpent from the Garden that comes to deceive by his cunning. It is refusing to put our doubt over and above His Word and offering up to the Lord once more the gift of our unguarded trust.

Renewed Faith Closes the Gaps

Inherent in Jesus' call back to first love is the call to repent of unbelief and come back to *first faith*. To believe and to trust Him as we did at first. To believe with childlike receptivity and unfettered confidence, as we did at first—before we were swallowed in the weight of all that came after. He calls us back to Himself, the One who alone is untouched and untainted by sin, age and the evil one's sway. Jesus never changed His perspective or drew back in His heart.

To go back is to repent of unbelief and come back to the place of trusting as we first did. Believing without drawing

85

back. Standing against the accuser with the truth of the everlasting Word, regardless of circumstance, personal deficiency or the opinions of others, including our own.

The Lord would say to us:

Come back to believing Me and taking Me at My Word. When you first believed, you received, and you let My love go deep. You fell headlong in love and ran headlong into abandonment. So, first come back to believing. Break your agreement with the lie that I have somehow changed. That I have altered My opinion or My heart's movement toward you.

Was I naïve when I spoke those things to your heart at first? Was I missing information? Was I somehow subject to change as the years unfolded? Was I young and immature and uninformed?

No. I am the unchanging and ageless One, and I know the end from the beginning. My words are true and everlasting. I am as jealous as I have been from the first day, and I see far more of you than you see of yourself. I never changed My mind! I am exceedingly difficult to turn away, for how great is My jealousy? But you must come after Me voluntarily.

Your loss of fervency isn't root, but fruit—and the root is unbelief. What happened? You quit believing what you first believed. Return to Me by repenting of unbelief and returning to openhearted trust in Me.

Responding to this entreaty from the Lord, we come to Him and say,

You delight in me. Sing it over me until all the condemnation and accusation is silenced. Only Your love heals my wounded soul. So today, with courage, I trust Your great affection for me. I believe, help me in my unbelief. I reach

in faith to receive, to trust that Your love is everlasting, undiminishing, untainted and unyielding. I offer up to You the gift of my unguarded trust. I accept Your tenderness toward me. You wash me here—with the water of Your Word. You nourish and cherish me with the grace and truth of Your love (Ephesians 5:28–33).

I choose to believe You. I arise in confidence again to call myself Your friend, Your beloved one. You have loved me as the Father loved You (John 15:9). Here I abide and live. I will not distance my heart in the defense that says You won't do what Your Word promises. I believe You. I believe You are the holy, uncreated, everlasting Word—the Maker and Sustainer of all things. Where else can I go? Only You have the words of life. I believe You. Oh, washing joy. I believe Your words are true! You loved me as the Father loved You (John 15:9). I'm looking into Your eyes—there are no lies there. No exaggerations. No shadow of turning. You are the beautiful Man of truth. The radiance of the glory of God shining in Your face. All is as You say.

Faith closes the gap—bridges over the doubts—as we hold fast to the Branch, to the Man, the Bridegroom, who loved us and gave Himself for us. Our ears hear His voice again, and our hearts rejoice at the sound (John 3:29). He is who He says He is. We put aside our doubts and set our eyes upon Him alone. He is the Fountain of living waters, the springing-up Well within, the quenching Waters that satisfy, the Treasure in the field, the Bread of heaven, the Good Shepherd who is not a hard taskmaster, but the Husband of our hearts and the Beloved of our souls.

Confidence in Love Again

In my youth, the preacher had quoted John the beloved's claim as "the one Jesus loved" and beckoned me through the Word of God to know personally that I am God's favorite, as John knew it (John 13:23; 21:20). I shuffled in my seat, uncertain. *Me? His favorite? How does this work? If you're God's favorite, how can I be also?*

But the Lord stepped in to convince me. I felt His gaze, singling me out and persuading me of His enjoyment over just little me. It was the fact that He waited for my voice and my song, and how not a soul could take my place, that arrested and finally convinced me. How could I give only a part of my heart to Him if He knows me and loves me this way? And if He waits for my voice, and if no other voice can take my place, how can I not lift it to Him? In those days, a little seed took root that changed me forever. It was the seed of confidence in love.

There's something of the human capacity that must know, must feel deeply that we're the beloved one. We know the ache as children toward our parents or in marriage toward our spouses. We want to be known deeply and loved in that knowing. We don't want to be average but the favorite. We must know in the depth of our being that He enjoys us, personally. He made us to feel that way, for not one of us did He create generically, and never does He love us impersonally. In fact, He never draws His eyes away from each one of us, and He is attentive to our every cry. In truth, He could not be more personal with each of us (Job 36:7; Psalm 34:15).

First love comes when the heart is awakened to believe and receive His delight and enjoyment over us, even in our weakness; and it is lost when we suffer from the sickness and the distance of distrust. When we draw back and quit fully believing that He truly loves and has pleasure over us today, we lose the life-blood of everything. This is where the war is won and lost: at the gut-level, present-tense believing in His affection for *me*. Jesus called it *abiding in His love*. We can't persevere through life's troubles and difficulties without it.

This is not the kind of "believing" that remains at the mental-assent level, but rather is both heart and mind arising in confidence before Him of our preciousness and beloved-ness—to know in our gut what it is to love and be loved by Jesus Christ. To lose this sense of our preciousness to Him is like losing the secret of courage, strength and perseverance. Second-guessing and hesitancy were never meant to reside in the inner garden, the holy place of communion with God.

When we lose touch of His delight in us, performance picks up its familiar patterns, and we slowly move away from the center of everything. There is something in us that thinks we are to grow up and move on, outgrowing such tender, personal delight. Yet that is just the irony of the deception. The only way to mature in love is to continually receive and abide in *His love* through every moment of our weakness and immaturity; through every harsh circumstance and every barrage of accusation from the enemy. Every step away from His enjoyment is a step backward in our growth in Him. Every step toward abiding in His love—back to confidence in His enjoyment of us, and that He waits to hear our voice—is a returning to the love we had at first. We come back to the wonder and joy of knowing and believing that we are beloved, a place we were never meant to leave.

It can be humbling to admit we have lost touch of it. It isn't prestigious to confess we have drifted from the basic heart-beat of everything. I know I hesitated to acknowledge, even to myself, that such a simple thing could be at the root of my disheartenment. *Of course, I know He loves me. That's my life message. Of course, I'm sure of His delight in me.* But these were stand-in confessions. They were mental assents but not bleeding-hearted affirmations.

And even though I might have lingered in that denial for a time, there were *signs*. There were *indicators* that this subtle interior distance from Jesus' cherishing love was, in fact, the culprit of the dampening—like when one song unexpectedly had me weeping for a few days straight. It was a simple song, describing the Lord standing and waiting for me at the end of the day, not disappointed or angry, but running toward me. Each time I would listen to it, I would weep, as though washed with truth that was restoring me. I had to ask myself, *Why is this wrecking me so?* The simplicity of the lyrics had my analytical pride wagging its head in disapproval. *Of course, I know these truths.* But my heart, having begun to reach out in hope and desire again, pushed the pride aside to run out to meet Him—the One whom the song described. The One whom I knew. The One who was not disappointed but running to meet me.

The Lord revives our love for Him as we repent of unbelief and return to trust and confidence in His love. This takes humility and breaking our agreement with the pride that gave birth to unbelief. Believing and then receiving His love are never hard for our hearts when we have humbled ourselves—when we have broken our agreement with unbelief and surrendered again to trusting. It's only hard when we're still walled up in pride. Jesus does not change the way He stands as a fork in the road between pride and humility. And just as at the very beginning of coming to Him in faith, trust and surrender, it's only the humble who receive Him all through life's pilgrimage. Only those who know their need can come to Him. *To come back to first love is to come back to humble receiving.* The pride of unbelief must be checked at the door, and only those with childlike trust, who gladly take up the cup of His mercy, can enter, drink and receive.

Jesus knows when our mental assents no longer match our gut-level experiences of His love. He doesn't pull back in surprise or disdain over these gaps, but rather orchestrates our lives to bring exposure of them, so that as we repent and return, the breaches might be closed.

As we repent of the ways we have entered unbelief, of the subtle agreements with lies we have entertained, our trust and confidence in Him is restored once again. We leave the cold and guarded mental assent of our heads and sink down into the warmth of His tender enjoyment and love in the depth of our hearts. And the gaps close. The tears wash. *He loves me. Oh, how He loves me*, we sing like we sang at first. He renews our youth, and the wonder of the Gospel makes us new again.

PRAYER

Jesus, I open my heart to You and ask You to show me any areas of unbelief, where I have quit trusting in You fully, or where my confidence before You in love has been threatened. I yield these areas to You and break my agreement with every untruth concerning Your heart and Your nature. Stir my love for You and my childlike trust in believing You as I return to You with my whole heart.

STEPS FORWARD IN KEEPING PASSION FOR JESUS

- Ask the Lord to highlight any areas where your trust and confidence in Him havve been injured. As He shows you these things, repent of your agreement with any distortions about Him that you have let in.
- Make an affectionate resolution to come back to child-like trust by telling Him what you know to be true about Him through His Word and even from your own testimony of His kind leadership over your life.
- Intentionally open your heart to Him to receive His tender delight over you personally, letting go of every

reservation in your heart and bringing down every wall of resistance or doubt by His enabling grace. With childlike faith, tell Him you believe He is who He says He is and that you are what He says of you, and that you willingly receive His love fully.

Setting Our Hearts toward the Wilderness Pathway

Together in a run-down Denny's restaurant, in a less-than-affluent part of town, my sister and brother and I sat across the table from a man whose passion for Jesus would mark me deeply and alter the trajectory of my days. College-aged triplets, now a long way from home, we sat there mesmerized, listening to him talk—chiming in every now and then with our best attempts to respond with feigned profundity.

I leaned in with rapt attention, conflicted. Part of me was listening to his words, floored and maybe intimidated by his sheer charisma. And part of me was terrified he might ask me a question I wouldn't know the answer to. Still, I'll never forget some of the things Mike Bickle said to us that day. Like a man pierced by wonder, he spoke of the vast treasury of the knowledge of God—a storehouse that I couldn't help but suspect he himself had already begun to find.

With his tattered Bible spread open on the table—a maze of highlighted words in every color, and lines and handwritten notes in every direction—he showed us from Proverbs 2:1–5 how we are invited to search and to find the knowledge of God. Tracing the verses with his finger, he spoke of treasuring God's Word through long and loving meditation, crying out with desperate hunger for wisdom and understanding and, most of all, searching for the knowledge of Jesus as though for hidden treasure, turning over every rock in this holy quest.

Mike wasn't giving us a teaching. He wasn't leading us in a Bible study or inspiring us for the day. Compelled himself on this pursuit of finding the vast riches of the beauty of Jesus, he was inviting us to come along on this rigorous but glorious path. The quest would mean years of searching, fueled by hunger and desperation, yet assured by the truth of God's desire to answer. It would be costly, would test us with its delays and would require of us perseverance when the path went crosscurrent to the values of quick impact and popularity. We would need the Lord to give the grace of ardent abandonment to Him in prayer, fasting and waiting before Him. But in the end, like the promise of the passage, we would find the most precious thing in all of heaven and earth: *the knowledge of the Man Christ Jesus.*

That day I understood there are vast riches the Father desires to reveal of His Son, but He gives these treasures based on our hunger. Whatever it is in the Lord that we find ourselves able to live without, we will go without. But that which we cannot live without—that which we pant after with hunger and seek with desire—we will in time have. He only gives to the hungry. He gives salvation freely, according to our need of mercy, but He gives the depths of the riches of the beauty of His Son— and we grow in intimacy with God—based on our appetite for Him. And the question before each of us, as those redeemed in Christ, is: How much of His beauty do we *desire* to see? How closely in love and friendship do we *desire* to walk with Him?

I caught a vision to search for the knowledge of Jesus like a covetous man searches after wealth, even forgoing some of the many good things along the path that I might lay hold of the *ultimate* thing. I understood, because we have limited capacities, there are always tradeoffs. And if we desire to be filled with the riches of the beauty of Jesus, relinquishing some of these secondary things is what makes way for inward hunger, space and capacity. And in that capacity, we would be filled with the greatest commodity we could possibly possess: intimacy with Christ Jesus. We would begin to burn with the fire of having tasted and seen Him; no longer echoes of things we'd only heard, but voices proclaiming the Man we had seen and known.

This desperate cry I heard in my early twenties tore open my heart and innermost being. It reached into my deepest holy longings and grabbed hold of them—causing me, in turn, to cry out for what I had never known was available in Jesus: the deep things of God. My eyes were opened to behold the vast treasury of His beauty, strengthening my inner being to make way for the indestructible love of Christ Jesus, in an intensity I'd never known possible.

The Lord tore my heart open, using a man who, though weak and broken, was burning for God. Something had laid hold of him so deeply, and each time I heard him preach, a burning cry for God broke forth from a heart. I was pierced by a vision to know the depths of God's beauty—a cry of holy passion. The Lord laid hold of my heart and evoked a profound groan in me, more than I had ever known before. God pierced me with a wonder that rearranged things deeply within me. Though Mike's words and passion for Jesus played a part in this awakening, it was *the Lord* who laid hold of my heart, impressing upon me just how compelling Jesus truly is.

When the Lord stirred my heart with this new thirst and passion for Himself, He elevated my vision in God to places I did not know existed. It awakened a level and depth of desire for Jesus that simply was not there before. And that new awakening reordered my days, my priorities, my time and my pursuits. Everything became centered around that holy love and preoccupation for the Man Christ Jesus. Nothing made sense unless it came under and served that highest, holy ambition of knowing Him fully—of knowing His heart and His love—and responding wholeheartedly without restraint.

Again, my heart was provoked in those days by what many of the men and women of history had known in intimacy, in friendship, in wholehearted sacrifice for Jesus. And a deep yearning arose within my spirit—a cry arising from a desire from which I've never recovered: *Why can't I know the riches of His beauty as the Word describes? Lord, I must know You!*

What I'd known of Him already was not enough. I yearned to respond and to become one unwilling to settle for anything but the depths of the true knowledge of God in my heart and the raging love for Him that springs forth from it.

Searching for Treasure

In the months and years that followed that conversation in Denny's, you could find me often in an empty, overgrown lot behind my duplex apartment, pacing back and forth, alone. Sometimes it was in my room, poring over my open Bible, hour by hour. And many evenings it was at the top of a hill, where I'd watch the sun close out the day in splendor. Waiting. Watching. Praying. Sometimes with tears. Sometimes with just the open spaces of quiet and stillness. Many times, boredom would surge, or doubt about the wastefulness of such hours would rise. Still, His invitation to search for Him as for treasure—the conviction of how *little* I truly knew Him, how *urgent* the hour I was living in and how *small* my capacity was to receive all that He desired to give a willing heart in holy love and understanding—fueled my seeking heart. I gave Him my time in prayer, my hunger in fasting, my strength poured out in waiting on Him, rather than producing something that men might esteem. With His call in my ear, I laid my "gold in the dust," my own dreams surrendered and men's opinions cast aside (Job 22:24; Lamentations 3:24).

Though my vision was high, I soon found the path often to be difficult. It was most often dry and barren—like a wilderness. As the metaphor of Proverbs 2 implies, searching for something like silver or gold is neither a quick nor an easy quest. I knew the promise that He rewards those who "diligently seek Him," but I had never pressed on it in a way that tested me and cost me something (Hebrews 11:6).

Many days felt mostly futile, like I'd spent my strength in vain. Where was the treasure? Where was the finding after searching? But then, to those inward wrestlings, I would recall: *I've already counted the cost of this tower, and I knew that days like this would be part of that cost* (Luke 14:28). And most of all, I would remember the desire of the Lord that first awakened my heart. I'd felt His beckoning to come, His desire to be known by His people, not superficially but deeply—to be surrendered to, not partially but wholly (Matthew 22:37). Nothing draws forth the heart like the desire of the Lord, and it was this that compelled me and sustained me, even in the difficulty of waiting (John 17:3, 24, 26).

Did He answer? Did I find Him? Was there really a treasure to be found in the knowledge of Jesus? A tasting that comes to the hungry who seek after Him and search for Him? Yes. Without question. It wasn't overnight, and it wasn't explicit, but progressively and subtly, my deepest affections began to be accessed and laid hold of by Jesus in the waiting of prayer and fasting. The fasting became a feasting, as it was always intended to be. The lesser things and small sacrifices that were laid aside made room for the most precious and satisfying pleasures available—experiencing the love and joy and all-satisfying delight of friendship with Jesus. My spirit began to taste and feast more and more upon the beauty of Jesus—through prayer and through long and loving meditation in His Word. I began to know and experience His love and to peer with wonder into the beauty of His Person.

The most transforming exchange in life is when we receive the knowledge of God into our hearts by the revelation God gives of Himself to our spirit. It changes our interior life, our wants and desires, and the core of who we are. The most pleasurable way we could possibly live is to make the knowledge of God our chief pursuit and ambition.

There is a mystery about finding the treasure and gaining the knowledge of Jesus. He has built humility into the finding of it. It is a humble road to know Him. We want to be vindicated for our long hours of prayer or our discipline, and He hides the reward from men's eyes. He wants our dreams to be not the impact we have but *He Himself.* He wants us to be vindicated or ultimately satisfied not by the revival that breaks out but by the gain of *Him.* He desires that we would be able to say as Paul, "But whatever gain I had, I counted as loss for the sake of Christ. Indeed, I count everything as loss because of the surpassing worth of knowing Christ Jesus my Lord. For his sake I have suffered the loss of all things and count them as rubbish, in order that I may gain Christ" (Philippians 3:7–8 ESV).

Our deepest affections are not easily accessed or won over. They are deep beneath the surface of our lives—like a rudder beneath the ship.[1] They take us places from day to day, but they do not get accessed quickly or effortlessly. We may have words and language that claim wholehearted love for Jesus. We may sing songs that declare our affections, and we may even feel those affections in measure. But our deepest passions are not so easily laid hold of or articulated. They are hidden from us. And though we sincerely desire to love Jesus with our all, we ourselves do not possess the power to conquer our own affections for Him. Only He possesses such power, and He is unlike other conquerors. He wants *voluntary* love. He refuses to take over our lives against our wills. He wants us willingly to draw near to Him, desirously to seek Him, to offer Him our hunger and time and the meditations of our hearts. He wants us to desire eagerly what He longs to bring forth in our lives.

Embracing the ache of hunger and making our way into the wilderness of prayer and fasting are how we partner with Him voluntarily in His quest to conquer fully our affections for Himself.

The Way of God Is the Wilderness

There's an old chorus we used to sing in the prayer room that went like this: "The way of God is the wilderness; it's always been the wilderness. The way of God is weakness, voluntary weakness."[2] I might not have had words for it in my earlier days, but when I carved out space and time and drew away in prayer and fasting, I was embracing a *wilderness*, comprised of a lifestyle of voluntary weakness.

Prayer is weak. Fasting is weak. Investing our time and strength in the secret place, instead of in that which produces something the world esteems, is weak. When we wait on the Lord in prayer, when we give up our time and set aside other plans, when we go without food because desire for Him has us wanting Him most, when we leave our to-do lists to pore over His Word, we sow our strength into the soil of what is unseen (Matthew 9:15; Galatians 6:8; James 5:7). We give up the fantasy of success before men for the dream of truly knowing Him deeply with the faith that says, "I know He rewards those who seek Him diligently."

Perhaps no other passage of Scripture lays out this invitation more clearly and directly than His Sermon on the Mount: the call to wholeheartedness as displayed through the eight Beatitudes and the lifestyle of prayer, fasting and giving. This lifestyle is the way forward in walking out our pursuit of wholehearted love and abandonment to God. We voluntarily leave the many influences of the world, of the busyness, of the cares of this life, in order to seek and find communion and fellowship with Jesus—to have our eyes filled with His beauty and our thirsting hearts quenched by delighting in Him. And by nature of the fact that we leave the clamor all around us to go into our rooms and shut our doors in the secret place before God, it is a place we each venture into, and must go into, *alone*. No one can go to this place for us. No one can respond to this call for us. Each one must himself venture into this wilderness to seek and find the Treasure, to acquire the oil of knowing his God (Matthew 25:4; Luke 12:34).

The Lord has always brought His people to the wilderness to meet Him and to leave every other affection. It was here that He desired to have fellowship and communion with the children of Israel, betrothing them to Himself. "Go and cry in the hearing of Jerusalem, saying, 'Thus says the LORD: "I remember you, the kindness of your youth, the love of your betrothal, when you went after Me in the wilderness, in a land not sown"'" (Jeremiah 2:2). It was to the wilderness that He called and met Moses, John the Baptist and Paul. He brings us to the wilderness to come and remember that man does not live by bread alone but by His Word (Deuteronomy 8:3). And though we may not go to an actual physical wilderness, the way of living characterized by fasting, prayer and giving that Jesus described in the Sermon on the Mount is one that could be called *a wilderness lifestyle*. Here we are stripped of all the lesser pleasures, our clinging to them exposed, and—if we respond to His beckoning—our friendship with the world severed (Deuteronomy 8:2; James 4:4).

Though not popular and in direct conflict with today's culture—both inside and outside the Church—this is a *voluntary wilderness*, this lifestyle that Jesus laid out in the Sermon on the Mount. It's a way of living in consistent prayer, regular fasting and simplicity of lifestyle so as to give more away, and it's thoroughly biblical and absolutely essential to knowing Jesus.

Can we find places of solitude where our hearts can begin the journey of the fire of transformation? Will we embrace the grace of fasting that Jesus freely offers to the hungry—a grace that takes our hunger and increases it?

We do this not to escape from the world but to actively resist its sway and seduction in our hearts. Illusive ties of friendship and allegiances to the world get severed here as we reach out of love for Jesus in prayer and fasting with desire for the most precious and holy friendship—the intimacy for which we were fashioned (James 4:4–5).

The wilderness of prayer and solitude and fasting is the place where we can draw aside from the influence of the world and give ourselves to the knowledge of the truth. It's the lifestyle that comes alongside our inward desires for Him and brings us to that glorious point of the end of ourselves and the discovery of Him. It makes space for Him as it brings us out of our busyness and frantic living, deepening our affections and sharpening our urgency—making big things big and small things small.

Inward transformation happens at this meeting place—this place of encounter with the Lord. All the lesser desires get stripped away, little by little, until He alone remains as our ambition (2 Corinthians 5:9). He draws us to this wilderness to find Him as our true treasure until our hearts can say in truth: "The LORD is my portion; therefore I will wait for Him" (Lamentations 3:24 NIV; Matthew 6:21 NIV). We begin to glory, not in our own various attainments, but in understanding and knowing Him (Jeremiah 9:23–24; 2 Corinthians 10:17).

In a culture where busyness and efficiency are so highly esteemed, this seeming "waste" of hours and attention and strength necessitates a deep inward resolve, fueled by holy affection and abandonment to God. With a multitude of distractions and many opportunities competing for our time, it will certainly cost us, as Jesus said it would. It might involve missing out on some ministry opportunities or other occasions, perhaps spending less time socially with friends or living more simply so we don't have to work as much. This isn't easy, but the internal rewards are incalculable. An ardent interior cry for the deepest intimacy with Christ must be the force behind these choices—a groan that we would no longer be restricted by our own affections but *freed* to enter the vast treasury of intimacy and friendship with Him for which He created us (2 Corinthians 6:12).

He Calls Us Back to the Wilderness

When Jesus calls us to return to Him, He, of course, puts His finger first on the heart of the matter and the motives deep within us. He draws us back to Himself, to the true starting place of His love and affection and never-waning passion. He draws upon the deep desires He first awakened in us and has never wavered in His plan to answer. He searches us for the hidden hindrances of unbelief, angst and distrust, and beckons us to the repentance that renews and pulls us to our feet again in expectant faith.

This returning, however, is more than coming back to His love again, desiring again and believing again. These are the deep, inward returnings—but there are *outward* paths as well. Whenever the heart is overcome with the love of Christ, pierced with desire born out of a tasting of the most satisfying One, interior achings give way to outward reachings. And the drawing of the Lord upon our hearts back to first love leads us to seek and find Him in the wilderness of prayer, of fasting, of waiting upon Him, of making space and time to hear His voice . . . *as we did at first.*

So, He calls us back. He beckons us to remember what we tasted of Him in the past. We tasted, and we saw that He was good (Psalm 34:8; 1 Peter 2:3). We found His love to be better than wine and His lovingkindness to be better than life (Song of Solomon 1:2; Psalm 63:3). The tasting was real. The drinking was real. Jesus is the most potent Person alive—the only actual Quencher of our innate thirsting. Yet with each satisfaction and slaking of our thirst, we simultaneously experienced a deeper aching and desiring for more of Him. The joy of finding Him is never neutral on our souls. Every unearthing of the treasure evokes a greater groaning. Both joy and mourning come with every taste. We experience both the joy of His beauty and the mourning over the gap of what our eyes have not yet seen, what we have yet to experience in Him and how we have yet to respond to Him fully.

> **Whenever the heart is overcome with the love of Christ, pierced with desire born out of a tasting of the most satisfying One, interior achings give way to outward reachings.**

He calls us back because the search was not over. The seeking of treasure was not finished—in fact, we've only just begun. We've seen only the edges of His beauty, and our glory is to keep searching for and unearthing the treasure until we finally see His face (Job 26:14; Proverbs 25:2). And then for all the ages to come, we will keep pressing in with endless desire for the inexhaustible beauty of His nature, His heart and His love. Yes, there have been delays and twists and turns we did not expect, but the aim remains the same: the upward call to know Him—an aim not attained passively but by diligent pursuit (Philippians 3:12–14; Hebrews 11:6).

The delays that we find in the life of faith may be counter to our culture, but they are prevalent in Scripture. The Lord is pleased by perseverance, by endurance in the waiting, with hearts set upon the promise of God, decade after decade— believing His Word is true and that He has not changed His mind. He describes saints who persevere in this way as those of whom the world is not worthy (Hebrews 11:38). Here He invites us.

He does not want us to be those who simply taste. He wants us to be those who can cry out as John did from the wilderness and say, "My joy is *made full* at the sound of the Bridegroom's voice!" (John 3:29).[3] Once again, the delays that we have faced along the way were not His denying our prayers, but the agents He sent to us to evoke in us an even greater panting and desperation—a greater leaving of the world and all its enticements—that we might be freed to experience the depths of joyful communion with Him.

Capacity for Beauty and Love

Love always involves capacity. We think we can take so much in and still have room for the Lord. Yet over and over, Jesus spoke of the inability for the heart to go in two directions. We cannot serve both God and money. We cannot have both friendship with the world and friendship with God. We cannot love Jesus in fullness and at the same time possess all the lesser clingings, lesser loves.

Though we were made with *endless* boundaries to know love and communion with God, we were never fashioned to do more than *one thing* with our affections. And whenever the heart is divided, its love is also impaired. Whatever it is that we give our time to, our attentions to, our thoughts to, this is what our treasure is and what fills up our interior space and chips away at our capacity, little by little. We might think of ourselves as desperately hungry for the Lord, but if our inward capacities are heaving with other things, even good things, we are not prepared to feast upon His beauty. We're not prepared to take in and be fully satisfied with superior pleasures.

We cannot have both friendship with the world and friendship with Jesus. There is a cost to find the treasure we were fashioned to unearth—a cost Jesus made no apologies for. He said the way was narrow, the cross we would bear was compulsory and the building of the tower would be costly. Finding the highest pleasure always necessitates a forsaking of the lesser. In order to find the true treasure of the knowledge of Jesus and have our hearts there with it, we must first sell all that we have to buy the field.

Thus, the question becomes: How much of His beauty do I want to see in this age of faith—the age before I see Him face-to-face? How far will He let me go in His grace in finding the depths of knowing Him? How much holy tasting of His goodness will He allow me to partake of? How filled with eternal pleasure, of delighting in Jesus and captivated by His beauty, can I be? Or, as the chorus inquires, "How far will You let me go? How abandoned will You let me be?"[4]

Few make the space that only hunger can forge and sit alone in the quiet where His voice is heard and the Treasure found. In our day, more than ever, with the deluge of media and inundation of noise, with the ability to mask all our imperfections, and with our hubristic habit of multitasking, we disdain the weak place of prayer, solitude and fasting. Yet it's *here* that the highest pleasures available to the human experience are found. The deep things of God, the discovery of the depths of His heart and personality, are available to us, and

> How much of His beauty do I want to see in this age of faith—the age before I see Him face-to-face? How far will He let me go in His grace in finding the depths of knowing Him?

we have not even conceived of the things He has prepared for us in revealing them (1 Corinthians 2:9, 10). We were fashioned to taste and see and experience the beauty of Jesus and to be ultimately satisfied with nothing else.

From this wilderness, Jesus stretches out His inviting hands in the middle of our clamoring world, and to the ones least likely to forsake all the stimulants, consumption and duty-juggling—to come seek Him and find Him (Matthew 7:7).

Do we desire to come after Him? Do we desire to enter the fullness of joy and the abundance of life for which He died to make a way? The Holy Spirit has searched the deep things of God and wants to give them to us (1 Corinthians 2:10). He has the Father's permission. He will give them to us according to our hunger and desire.

If we will venture into the wilderness of prayer and solitude, making room for hunger, He will satisfy. Wherever He finds hunger in us, He answers with tastes and satisfactions, swelling with greater thirstings that mark us forever. The tastes are both sweetness and deeper yearning for more. They are the sort of pleasurable longing that C. S. Lewis described as the sweetest thing in all his life—the longing to reach the Mountain, to find the place from whence all the beauty came.[5]

Jesus is never so sweet as when He is waited for with the achings of hunger. It's always the hungry that He answers, the longing heart that He fills with good things (Psalm 107:9; Matthew 5:6). Here He brings us to the place where we can finally say with authenticity: *Nothing is more precious to me than Him.* Favor of man and success in the eyes of the world can come and go. We are already answered in the deepest place. If we will carve out time, He will reward with the riches of His beauty. If we will respond to His desire with voluntary weakness, He will answer our desire to see and know Him (John 17:24; Psalm 27:4). But not only that. If we will bring His Word back to Him in prayer, until we've indeed tasted of its sweetness profoundly, we will begin to speak words that carry weight—a source of strength and deliverance to the hearer. We will be able to truly strengthen others, for it is here that any word we would ever speak about Him to others is filled with the weight of true encounter.

He desires to fill His people to such a measure that their mouths proclaim His sweetness, a proclamation that can *only* arise from having first made space and capacity through panting for Him (Psalm 42:1). We begin to speak of what we've seen and known, inviting others to the feast of that which we've tasted in Jesus and found so precious (Psalm 34:8; 119:103).

The hour we live in is indeed urgent. There is a Man—who is God, the Lord—with a soon return and a heart that refuses to come back to a dull and indifferent bride. And the Man is watching and inviting us. He waits for our response.

There's a path before our feet called *voluntary weakness*, and the invitation is wide open. The way is narrow and hardly impressive (Matthew 7:14). It includes sowing seeds to where we cannot see, only with the eyes of faith perceiving the worth of those offerings (James 5:7). But His Word cannot lie. He says, "Everyone who thirsts, come to the waters. . . . Listen carefully to Me, and eat what is good, and let your soul delight itself in abundance. Incline your ear, and come to Me. Hear, and your soul shall live" (Isaiah 55:1–3). And though the landscape of our day boasts of challenges that generations before have not yet seen, the wisdom of His Word invites us to the same path it has always prescribed: *voluntary weakness*—the path that leads us headlong into His strength and beauty (Psalm 27:4; Matthew 5–7; Luke 10:42).

This is the wilderness of first love and the way we return to first love. We've been there before, and He calls us back again. To go to the wilderness requires a willingness to leave all that is behind again and to forge back into the place of barrenness with no certainty of what the future will hold—only that He is our future, our aim, the dream of our lives.

This wilderness is not a pit stop—a place we go to in order to get to the next place. It is not meant to be used for the gain of something men might applaud. It is to be entered with the escorts of love and desire for the real Person and pursued by those who refuse to be comforted by anything other than Him (Psalm 77:2). Those willing to go to the wilderness, running after their Beloved Jesus, must come with the singular aim of finding *Him*. He is their future, and He is their reward.

PRAYER

Jesus, here I am before You. I confess that I want to make capacity for more of You in my life. I want You more than all the other things, and I know that finding the Treasure of knowing You requires walking the wilderness pathway of prayer, fasting and givenness to meditation upon Your Word. I ask for Your grace as I set my heart toward this wilderness pathway. You are my dream. You are my delight.

STEPS FORWARD IN KEEPING PASSION FOR JESUS

- The first step in setting your heart toward the wilderness pathway of prayer and fasting, the paths beneath keeping first love, is embracing a willingness to miss out on a few things—be it opportunities, events or a sense of success by what the world esteems valuable—in light of the gain you will find in Christ. Each time you choose the wilderness pathway and "miss out" on something, tell Jesus, "My heart is Yours. Anything that may feel like a loss is worth it to be near You and to know Your heart."

- Carve out time in your schedule for prayer and set your heart toward a lifestyle of consistent weekly fasting, all motivated by lovesick yearning for Jesus. Mark dates and times in your schedule you can devote specifically to prayer. What you schedule will be more likely to happen. Also determine a day or a meal that you will choose to fast each week.

- Ask the Lord to strengthen your faith and perseverance in this pathway through the understanding that dry times in prayer will come, your reaching will at times feel fruitless, but God's Word is *true*, and He rewards those who diligently seek Him (Hebrews 11:6).

Enduring God's Loving Chastening in Our Friendship with Jesus

The sputtering fire in my fireplace struggled to push back December's cold as I hovered over pages of teaching notes, preparing for a Bible school class in a few hours. It had been a while since I'd taught this particular section from Song of Solomon 3, a lecture titled "Divine Chastisement." Maybe it had also been a while since I had really taken to heart these biblical truths—how the Lord disciplines those He loves and how we often mistake such chastening as His disappointment in us rather than His love for us.

I reached for the book *The Chastening of God* by a man whom I esteem beyond words, my dear friend Bob Sorge. And while I thumbed through its pages, that day's teaching preparation took a back seat to my own heart being taught—and reminded—of the way Jesus leads us. Some months before, I had journaled my prayers of "Jesus, it's too much." I had felt my heart's inability to move in joy and trust and passion as it had at first. But I didn't know what went wrong or how to return. Now, without warning, through Bob's words and the witness of his life, lights began flashing in my understanding as to how the Lord's hand of chastening might presently be leading my own story and life.

Bob doesn't mince words or gloss over painful realities, and he writes with a grit that makes the heartache of the reader start to nod with a sense of feeling known. Bob's words on the page described how the Lord redemptively uses adverse circumstances to correct and discipline His children for their progress and maturity. With candid and direct articulation, Bob explained that, in this process of the Lord's chastening, He even *lames us*, leaving us limping. Bob described the response God looks for from us in His loving discipline of His sons and daughters (Hebrews 12:3–15):

> Don't let the lamed member just hang and atrophy. Wrap the brace around the thing, gather your strength, and continue to hobble your way forward.
>
> How does God want us to respond to chastening? He wants us to keep moving, even if it's with a hobbling limp. We'll be healed as we stay in the race. . . . Don't give up! God has a purpose. Get back in there, and finish the race! You'll be healed as you run. . . .
>
> Satan participated in the chastening because he had an agenda to turn you into a casualty, but God's agenda is to make you a mighty end-time weapon in His hand. Your first response is to collapse. But when you move one finger, even slightly, and make the smallest movement with your hand, heaven gets excited. . . . When you refuse to crumple to the ground, but brace your knees and shakily stand again to your feet, heaven watches with even more excitement. "Look at her! She's still standing. We just might have another one!"[1]

Tears began to stream from my eyes as I took the truths in, a new perspective hovering like light suspended over a dense fog, beginning to break it open. I felt as though my heart—touched by hope—was rushing out ahead of me, and I was limping along behind it, a bit reluctant but, at the same time, desperate to believe.

And with the eyes of my heart reaching in faith, I turned and looked behind me into the years past—the twists and turns that we had experienced in our nearly two decades of ministry and relationships. Along with so many blessings were also the numerous rigors and difficulties, the confusion of the many opinions of the *mad, glad and sad*, the heartache over those who'd been hurt and sometimes rightly so, the fear of failing in unknown ways, the doubts over the inarguable deficiencies of weak people, of *myself*—all like chapters of a book of which I'd been anxiously searching for the titles.

What happened? Who was to blame? Was it the attack of the enemy? Was it my own deficiencies? Was it the weaknesses or failures of the people around me? What happened, God?

He chastens those He loves for the sake of friendship and intimacy with Himself.

For so long, I'd been wrestling to understand, to make sense of the turbulence and what seemed at times like unraveling I had seen, to have some sort of clarity on all that was behind me, all that had transpired. Moving into the future with hope and joy is tightly knit to right perspectives on the past—the ability to see the hand of the Lord and His leadership in a way that makes the heart rest in peace and security.

That understanding came suddenly, in a moment's time, like I'd been given a truth that wiped all my previous conclusions and chapter titles clean. One heading trumped all the lesser contributing subtitles: *Friendship.* It was all about friendship *with Jesus*—the greatest desire and deepest prayer of my life.

This singular title was needed—and all the chapters came under it, rising above all the lesser captions.

He chastens those He loves for the sake of friendship and intimacy with Himself. Yes, there were other players and other contributors in the struggle and in the unfolding years—the enemy and his ploys, my sin and deficiencies, the sin and faults of others, the circumstances of a broken and fallen world. But these could not take the lead as the primary drivers of the storyline. He is over and above all of these in His sovereign direction of my life. Every other contributor bends the knee to Him. And in that moment, I understood that His overarching leadership was to use all of these subplots for the sake of friendship with Himself.[2]

The Cost of Friendship with Jesus

Another phrase from Bob's writing that went through my spirit was this: *You don't know what you ask for.* And with that phrase, I remembered all the lamentations and all the groans that I'd prayed—the desires of my heart with which He had wounded me. That He would open my eyes with "the spirit of wisdom and revelation in the knowledge of" Christ (Ephesians 1:17–19). That He would enlighten my heart to see the beauty, the splendor, the majesty of the Man Christ Jesus. That He would strengthen me with might in the inner man to know and comprehend the height, the width, the length and the depth of His love—to be filled with the very fullness of God (Ephesians 3:16–20). That I would love Him with all my heart, soul, mind and strength (Matthew 22:37).

I remembered all of these deepest prayers, like cries that had disrupted my whole life and set me on a track of mourning for that gap to close, of hungering and thirsting for that righteousness to be realized (Matthew 5:4, 6). These sincere expressions of grief for biblical Christianity left within me a gaping sense of disappointment as life unfolded and they remained unanswered.

To these groans, Jesus spoke now: *Do you know what you ask for?*

Then the light of understanding filled my heart. These are costly prayers. Their answers do not come to the casual cry. They are not prayers that are satisfied easily or quickly, but with pursuit and perseverance, over decades. And even more than that, the answers to these prayers necessitate a preparation. Jesus desires to answer them more than anything—for they were born in His heart from before time. But He will not bestow them upon an unreadied heart, lest the very weight of their answer destroy the intercessor. They cannot come to a flimsy soul, but to one strengthened with might in the inner man, one rooted and grounded in love, having undergone the testing of His chastening, the enduring of His discipline (Ephesians 3:16).

It is so easy to know this about the Lord and the way He leads us in love, but then to forget it as we experience it through the unfolding years or the troubling circumstances. The years of silence are part of His answer to us. The delays, the relational difficulties, that which seems to be grating against our ability to stand very well might be the hand of the Lord. Even the trials that come crashing in, blindsiding us—are we willing to consider that these, too, may very well be the greatest kindness of the Lord to access our deepest heart and answer our most holy prayers?

In direct opposition to the accusation with which we might wrestle—that He does not act in response to our prayers—He takes our prayers *so seriously* that He orchestrates our lives to position us for the answer. *The supreme principle of His sovereign directing of our lives is unto the actual answering of the prayers and groans that He has put within us.* They are the loving discipline and refining that He gives to those He loves.

Did we think we could pray such prayers and have Him stand aloof? Does He not avenge His own elect who cry out to Him day and night (Luke 18:7)?

It is the Lord Jesus being Himself to answer such prayers, costly as the answers may be. It is performing the very desires and intentions of His heart to answer them, for they came first from His own groanings. Yet to answer them, He would have to first refine us. He loves His people too much to fulfill our prayers without also giving us the very preparation needed to receive the answers.

When we want the Lord to come, we often forget that His coming necessitates a work of preparation in us so that the coming will not crush us in the end. It is to the one who has been lamed by His discipline, now standing and walking forward—though even with hands hanging down—who is prepared now for what he has prayed, that he might *see the Lord* and not be overcome.

When the Lord pressed upon my heart, *Do you know what you ask for?* He might as well have inquired, *Will you still ask? Are you willing to keep asking, even after the testing?* For with the understanding I received that these chapters behind me were titled "Friendship," and every part of the story had been unto that sovereign end and purpose, I also understood that He longed for His people to endure testing and walk forward, believing, and continuing to cry out for His promises. He was inviting me—as He invites all of us—to come out of these wilderness years of testing with a confidence that trusts His leadership, recognizing the profit promised to our souls and the certainty of the healing and good fruit He vows to bring to those trained by it (Hebrews 12:11).

And now, with the same desires but a tested love, I prayed:

I'll meet You in the wilderness again. And this time I will not pray naïve prayers—though the words may be the same. You warned me that the prayers were costly, and I answered so readily, "Of course, I still desire You to come!" And You pressed again: Do you know what you ask for?—all the while beckoning me with holy desire to keep asking. For rarely do You find those not only willing to pray the prayers of "Let me see Your face," but willing to be refined by the fire that buys the gold and gives the preparedness necessary for You to come in and dine with Your friends (Revelation 3:14–22).

The Means to a Glorious End

There are real times in our journeys of faith that the Lord's hand has seen fit to weaken us in the way, to tear and wound us, to refine and prune us, as He always does for His own. Did we expect something else? Yes, there is an accompanying great warfare and assault, a contribution of my own deficiencies and even stumbling; there is the added element of the wrongdoing of others around me, and even all the painful circumstances because of living in a fallen world with no person to blame. Yet each of these contributors are not *supreme*, and none of them could have a role without the nod of the One seated above, the great Shepherd and Overseer of our souls (1 Peter 2:25).

Without any whitewashing, the writer of Hebrews described the discomfort of the chastening He gives—even acknowledging that no discipline seems joyful in the present, but painful (Hebrews 12:11). Yet for the sake of our own profit, in His love for us and in His zeal that we would partake of Him in His holiness—the qualification for *seeing Him*—He disciplines the son He loves (Hebrews 12:10–11). He chastises His own, and a good son receives that discipline as part of the Lord's loving leadership and care, without giving way to despising it or becoming discouraged by it (Hebrews 12:5–6, 15).

This chastening of the Lord is not the end of the story, as it would seem. This discipline is not the end of our path, as discouragement can whisper. It is the Lord's means of bringing us to the glorious end that is our promised future. That wonderful end is sure: *He will also heal* (Hosea 6:1; Hebrews 12:13). He has torn us, but He will heal us. He has chastened us, but afterward, we will be restored and bear the fruit of righteousness. Thus, when we find ourselves limping, torn and broken under His hand of chastening, the storyline is not over, and His answer to our heart's cries to know Him and to see Him, to enter into the fullness that He would give the human heart in the age of faith, is not *no.*

Rather, the silence and the delay, the painful circumstances along the path that test and wound, are all servants to His greater purpose. They are meant to purify us for the purpose of greater love.

He will, in fact, answer our prayers even through the means of these troubles—if we receive and respond to Him rightly in them. If we have made our lives about Him—considered Him the gain, though we lose all else, making Him our boast and that which we consider the aim of our lives—then these chastening seasons, and even all the trials we undergo, work to produce that holy ambition in us. We endure the discipline and subject ourselves to our Father, and these difficult trials become His preparatory agents to ready us for the dream of our hearts: friendship with Him—the very answer to our prayers. Having this perspective frees us to live as Paul described:

> We rejoice in our sufferings, knowing that suffering produces endurance, and endurance produces character, and character produces hope, and hope does not put us to shame, because God's love has been poured into our hearts through the Holy Spirit who has been given to us.
>
> Romans 5:3–5 ESV

Without exception, all testing and suffering are invitations to greater intimacy with Jesus. Every season of pain we encounter can be received as a summons from God to know Him in a greater way. There is no intrinsic value in pain, and it is important to understand that God hates pain, sickness and suffering. His plan is to forever judge and vanquish it. So, we contend against the adversary and sickness while, at the same time, we receive the chastising that such circumstances bring to our souls, saying *yes* to the invitation of greater friendship and intimacy with Jesus that these escorts bring. We say with the psalmist, "It was good for me to be afflicted so that I might learn your decrees. . . . I know, LORD, that your laws are righteous, and that in faithfulness you have afflicted me" (Psalm 119:71, 75 NIV).

Coming Out Like Gold

There is a crushing, a dark night, and a testing that our voluntary love for Jesus must undergo. Love made worthy of the Lamb is love that has known the absolute weakening in the way, the crushing of the rose. Our misconceptions of the Lord's leadership over our lives are not neutral. We most often do exactly what Hebrews 12 corrects us for: We forget that the Lord leads our lives in this way. And in that forgetting, in these seasons of divine chastening, we either assume our adverse circumstances are not from the Lord's hand, dismissing this trial as coincidence, or we despair in the midst of it, forgetting that His testing is for our good, for the purpose of our healing so that we might come out—as gold (Job 23:10; Hebrews 12:5–6).

But the Lord is not so shortsighted nor shallow as we are. He wants everlasting partnership with an equally yoked bride, and He wants our deepest agreement with His purpose and ways. He wants us not only to pray the prayers He prays, but to be made ready for their fulfillment.

We often start out with "right" prayers, but we don't realize how insubstantial their root systems are. Then, when He leads our lives in such a way so as to answer these prayers, fashioning us as a potter molds clay or a refiner purifies gold, we faint with discouragement rather than zealously partner with His good leadership. We misinterpret His chastening as rejection, His tender compassionate leading as indifference, rather than seeing it is His most tender and passionate leading of our lives. He cannot answer our lofty prayers without making us ready for the answer. To do so would mean the probability of its destroying us with its pressure and weight.

The Lord desires friends. He wants our loyalty to be so deep that, when no one is looking, we are faithful to Him. We are living before an audience of One. We are to be as true to Him when no one is watching as when a multitude is watching, because we are truly living for *Him*, and He is enough. There are times in our lives when He leads as the refiner's Fire, as the disciplining Father, as the pruning Gardener—that He might bring us forth not only as those redeemed by His blood, but as those refined by His fire and proven worthy, as those chastened by His testing and qualified.

> **The Lord desires friends. He wants our loyalty to be so deep that, when no one is looking, we are faithful to Him.**

He is the God who lays hold of the affections of His people, stirs their desires, causes them to yearn for Him, evokes a burning groan within them for the very things that He desires to do—so that we might join Him in agreement and intercession as those who know the desires of His heart. He faithfully leads our lives to prepare us and make us ready for His answer—for His coming. Like Job, we are unprepared for when He Himself comes and answers us (Job 42:1–5). We think we are ready for what we ask, but only the One who searches our minds and hearts knows our true preparedness. He knows the way we take, and when He has tested us, we will come forth as gold (Job 23:10).

The severity of our circumstances can seem like He has gone too far. Are we willing to view them as the wisdom of God's leadership? To see them as the least severe means of bringing forth the full fruition of His love and will for us? What if the hardest blows were actually the gentlest means to unearth the inward giants that stand opposed to Him?

We look at our outward circumstances and deem them too severe. But the Lord alone knows our adversaries within. Only He knows what assignment He has before us and how far He is willing and wanting to take us in His grace if we will embrace the necessary preparation. Only He knows the abundance of fruit that He zealously wills to bring forth from us as we yield to Him in this pruning. He doesn't give harsher testing than is needed. He will never say, "I went too far with that purifying." He leads with precision and perfection, according to a mercy and kindness that surpasses the heavens.

The most precious and costly love is the love that is tested and found true. Words swelling with affection are no match for devotion proven by sacrifice. Jesus' love for you and me was not kept secret; it did not remain only lofty words. He demonstrated it. That which was within the heart of God was wrenched open and laid upon the cross. As the furnace refines silver and gold, the severity of the testing Christ endured brought forth the fierce streaming light of His love, so pure and potent.

Had Job died before his testing, he would have died a righteous man—rich in possessions and ease of circumstance, yet righteous nonetheless. But the testing he endured emptied him of all things, leaving nothing save a burning righteousness that was thereafter marked with the irrevocable scars of *provenness*.

When we lift our eyes to look just beyond this short life, toward that very real day when we will meet the eyes of *the Lamb slain for love*, something within us longs for the rewarding honor and fellowship of love not only *spoken* but *proven*. We long for love offered not only amid the ease of our culture and its surplus, but out of the grip of love's voluntary sacrifice.

May we count it a privilege to have our love for Him laid bare, tried and refined as gold. May we consider it pure joy in whatever we face or endure that, on the day we see Him, our many sincere words will be undergirded with a love tested and found true, an affection proven and shown genuine.

What He Is After in the Refining

Jesus is strategic in His leadership of our lives, of our secret history in Him, of our desires that He cultivates in us. First love always begins with Him—we love because He first loved—and thus, it is a sovereign and irrevocable marking. Likewise, the path forward, until the day He faithfully finishes the work He began in us, is also under His attentive and sovereign leadership.

He knows the future, knows the twists and turns ahead, knows the testing we will face. None of these are *diversions* from the ultimate end He has purposed for us. And do we play a part? Absolutely. Our voluntary agreement with Him, even when we do not understand what He is doing, is essential. He will not force us down these paths. His inheritance from the Father is not a robotic people in obligatory obedience, but a Bride that burns with voluntary love and agreement with Him, partnering with Him out of authentic affection and chosen loyalty.

> If Jesus doesn't chasten His Bride, she will be too immature and shallow in her experience to partner with His end-time purposes. Her chastening, therefore, will be her training ground. She will come to understand and appreciate the kindness, reasonableness, and necessity of God's end-time judgments.[3]

Jesus comes to each of us, and we meet His eyes again. By faith, we look into the eyes of the Author and Finisher of our faith, who, for the joy set before Him, endured the cross. We consider Him who endured such hostility lest we become weary and discouraged in our souls. Perhaps we have forgotten the way He leads—that He chastens every son whom He receives. Again, it is for our profit, that we might be partakers of His holiness. He disciplines and purifies us. And He is looking for our endurance. These oppositions are intended by the Lord to strengthen our faith, not to shatter it. Faith cannot grow without resistance. He is asking us if we will strengthen the hands that hang down and the feeble knees, weakened by the chastening. He invites us to walk forward even from this place, that we might enter into the healing, preparedness and holiness that He was always after (Hebrews 12:2–13).

It is critical that we understand that first love must be tested to become mature and worthy of the Lamb. Sincere love and response to Him at the beginning are crucial, but the cross we must bear to show forth and purify that love is also essential. That testing and chastening happens in real, actual circumstances, with real people and real disappointments. It happens with swift and blasting troubles and long, drawn-out delays. There are many tools that the Lord has at His disposal, but we are seldom prepared for how natural and seemingly disconnected from the bigger story these can seem to us when they play out in our everyday lives. This is why a perspective of His ultimate purpose must always be held in view.

He is after our good, and it is for our profit. He is after completion of what He began in us (Philippians 1:6). He is after a glorious Church, without spot or wrinkle or any such thing, holy and without blemish (Ephesians 5:27). He is after an abounding love in us, sincere and without offense (Philippians 1:10). He wants to count us worthy of this calling that He might be glorified in us and us in Him (2 Thessalonians 1:11–12). He is after the qualities of first love—zeal and tenderness, childlike trust and openhearted abandonment—in the state of mature love, having been tested, refined and proven.

Not only is our faith renewed as unbelief is repented of and renounced, but our zeal is stirred once more. When the power of unbelief is broken and the snare of disillusionment, cynicism and bitterness is thrown off, a renewed zeal—like we had at first—rises up in us. Like those who have just escaped a prison, we run forward with a renewed resolve, like never before, to lay hold of the promises of God before us. Like the writer of Hebrews exhorts, "We are not of those who draw back to perdition, but of those who believe to the saving of the soul" (10:39). With this resolve, we again press on in the race, making straight paths for our feet, being vigilant to war against any root of bitterness that might cause us to draw back from our futures and our callings (Hebrews 12:14–15).

With revived faith, we press on "to lay hold of that for which Christ Jesus" laid hold of us (Philippians 3:12). We partner with Him unto the fullness of transformation, that He would have His way and be fully pleased with His inheritance in us. He has laid hold of us at first that He might bring us into that fullness. We move forward, fueled by the unfettered faith that leaps in childlike trust once again. We trust Him even when we don't understand the circumstances. We commit our way to Him and rest in knowing that He leads according to love and with our highest good in mind. He will do what He has promised to do. He will finish the work He has started.

Deepened Friendship with Him after the Chastening

As His Body and His Bride, we must know that He surrounds our path and fills our way with every opportunity and every means possible to help us respond to Him and to say *yes* to Him in fullness. He uses the least severe means to accomplish the greatest amount of good in us—to bring us forth "holy and without blame before Him in love" (Ephesians 1:4). In His jealousy over each of us, He orders our lives in such a way that, as we respond to Him and to His grace, we come short in no gift, and what He began in us is brought to full completion (1 Corinthians 1:7; Philippians 1:6). Once again, He will not force us against our will. He desires partnership. He beckons the voluntary heart forward—that our testimony would be one of holy choosing and not mechanical submission. Now we can hear His voice resounding:

> I counsel you to buy from Me gold refined in the fire, that you may be rich; and white garments, that you may be clothed. . . . As many as I love, I rebuke and chasten. Therefore be zealous and repent. Behold, I stand at the door and knock. If anyone hears My voice and opens the door, I will come in to him and dine with him, and he with Me.
>
> Revelation 3:18–20

Though chastening is never enjoyable, but painful, it is a very real and necessary aspect of the Lord's loving leadership over His people, individually and corporately. He knows what we do not know about our own conditions. He sees to the heart. He knows the true state of our spiritual lives. And like the church of Laodicea, we can unwittingly believe we are rich when we are poor. We can inadvertently assume we are wealthy and in need of nothing when we are, in fact, naked and blind. We are beloved to Him, and He loves us too much to leave us spiritually shallow and blind. Lovingly, He disciplines us that He might ultimately answer our deepest longings to be fully His.

The chastening is not for our hurt, but unto our healing, unto our being clothed with white garments and made rich in God with the gold that remains (1 Peter 1:7).

Knowing that it is because of His deepest love for us as His children that He disciplines us, we receive these chastenings with a grateful heart. He has not left us to ourselves. He has come to move us closer to Him, ushering us into a greater holiness. Responding to Him with hearts of tender reception is what prepares us for the more extreme troubles upon the horizon that will come in increasing severity as His return draws near. Troubles will surely increase, and the love of many will grow cold, but the Lord seeks to preserve our hearts in those future testings by readying us through His disciplines and giving us right perspectives of these trainings, now (Matthew 24:6, 12; Hebrews 12:6).

Jesus beckons us to respond to Him in a humble and receptive way, submitting to His leadership as good and right and trustworthy. Having left behind the biting unbelief that was wounding our confidence and souring our perspective, He invites us to now receive His chastening hand upon us and to buy from Him gold, refined in the fire (Revelation 3:14–22). This gold is the most vital commodity we could possibly possess. It is the genuine relational knowledge of the Man Christ Jesus, and of His beauty—tenderizing and filling the heart with holy delight and indestructible joy.

He has yet so far to take us in Him. He gives grace to the humble, and to those who submit to Him in this, He draws near. To those willing to bow low in humility, recognizing their spiritual poverty, and to zealously buy from Him gold refined in the fire, He comes and knocks. A greater depth in friendship with Him—the very prayer and longing of our hearts—He invites us into today (James 4:7–8; Revelation 3:19–20). He wants friends of the Bridegroom who carry His desires close to their hearts. Having their joy made full in Him, they have no greater pleasure than to see Him receiving His full inheritance in His Bride. He wants to share these deep desires and fellowship, giving us grace to partner with Him in love and intercession for the fruition of His full inheritance to come forth in mature beauty and glory, as the Father ordained. He wants to bring us into this deep friendship with Him that causes us to turn and look at His Bride, to see her with His own eyes, loving her as He loves and saying of her, even in her brokenness and weakness, "Isn't she lovely? Isn't she beautiful?"

With such tender and jealous affection, Jesus calls us each by name. He knocks on the door of our hearts. If we hear His voice and open the door, He will come in and dine with us. We will sit at the table and dine with Him in the sweetest of friendship and intimacy, so much deeper than ever before. As we resist Satan and repent of our doublemindedness, He will lift us up. As we sever and repent of our friendship with the world—those ties exposed through the discipline of His loving hand—He will draw near to us and offer us deeper friendship with Himself than we've ever known.

He will sit at the table of our hearts, dining and feasting in relationship and love, a depth of communion only made possible by the training of His chastening. A partaking of holiness that He brought for our profit through the disciplining— that our eyes might be opened in revelation to see Him and that we would know unhindered friendship and communion with His heart (Hebrews 12:7–12; James 4:1–10; Revelation 3:19–20).

We will sit across the table from the One who loved us too much to leave us spiritually poor. And our hearts will burn within us, with a refined, fervent love—a love that "many waters cannot quench" (Song of Solomon 8:6–7).

His Delight Maturing Our Love in Times of Disruption and Difficulty

Jesus leads our lives in such a way as to disrupt us at times in order that we might be deepened in this comprehension of His tenderness toward us. He does not shy away from allowing times of divine discipline and shaking in our lives to bring us to this ultimate end (Hebrews 12:3–11; Revelation 3:19). The Lord shepherds His people this way. As He spoke of Israel to the prophet Hosea, there are times when He hedges our way with thorns, so to speak, so that we no longer chase other loves. He speaks tenderly to us in our disrupted condition, after He exposes us and strips us of secondary comforts. Then He speaks His cherishing love to our hearts, and His words penetrate our hearts like never before (Hosea 2:7, 14).

He uses times of disruption to shift us, uproot our false comforts, to expose our spiritual shallowness, and ultimately to lay us open for the profound eternal gain of greater depths of knowing Him and His beauty (Revelation 3:18–20). He disciplines us in His love for us by exposing our root systems for their faultiness. Then we see our spiritual shallowness and our lack of love for one another. It is not that He is disappointed in us, but that His tender love refuses to leave us in a place less than the fullness of His grace. He wants to carry to completion the work He began in us, causing our love to abound still more in knowledge and discernment (Philippians 1:6, 9). In these times, we are left vulnerable and raw, under an ever-intensifying exposure. We find ourselves saying, "Lord, I didn't see my sin, my lack of love." Yet it is here that Jesus wants to speak to us, straight to the heart, with words of tenderness. He shifts and disrupts us for this very purpose.

We cannot underestimate the power of knowing Jesus' delight in us and of having confidence in His love. Whether we have grown distant by trivializing it or by subtle unbelief, the Lord beckons us to enter in as never before. The Lord invites us to take our place at the banqueting table, by feeding on His Word and the truth of His love and delight over us. He beckons us to make this truth the meditation of our hearts all through the day (Song of Solomon 2:4). He calls us to enter into our great inheritance of delighting in His affection and being satisfied by the superior pleasure of knowing Him.

This sweetness is an inestimable source of strength to the heart and our way forward in maturing in love and wholeheartedness before Him, individually and together. Through it, we will endure hardship with grace, overcome offense and prevail over disappointment. As the sweetness courses through our hearts, minds and emotions, we will refuse bitterness and resist temptation. When we stumble along the way, it will be the source of strength for us to overcome every shadow of compromise, to resist shame and condemnation and to rise up in confidence before God, pressing forward in renewed holy pursuit of Him. Many would not connect the continual abiding in the tender affections of Jesus to be the source behind full givenness to Him in holiness, but this is the source for our abandonment.

As we experience this delight, we are freed to overcome areas of sin and compromise, maturing in holiness that overflows in highest joy, and we are catapulted forward by holy desire for one more taste of Him. One more sight of His beauty. One more experience of His love and joy. With hearts ruined for all the lesser pleasures, we cry out, "How far will You let me go? How abandoned will You let me be?" We lose our taste even for a misused word that might quench His Spirit or a selfish action that gets in the way of our heart's full experience of deep fellowship with Jesus, the Beloved of our souls.

This tender, cherishing love is how the Lord will mature His Church, His Bride, unto the glorious future the New Testament proclaims. It will be the escort into an unspeakable tenderizing of our hearts in love for one another. As we drink of His love and experience the joy of loving Him, it is a glorious foretaste of the Marriage Supper of the Lamb. It is the potent consolation that fills our souls and empowers us to yield fully to Him in every area of our lives. Again, it gives us the tenderness of heart to overflow and love one another—even our enemies—with the same love (John 17:24–26; Revelation 19:7).

Carrying and abiding in this sweetness of friendship and intimacy with Jesus, we will burn and overflow with the love and joy that John spoke of (John 3:29; 15:11). We will move forward together into the fullness the Father longs to give us. Throwing off every restraint and casting off all sin and compromise out of our desire to touch the highest things in Jesus' heart, we will be strengthened to run the race with endurance, for the prize of the excellence of knowing the Man Christ Jesus (Philippians 3:8–14). At every turn, this cherishing love will fuel our way forward, strengthening us in the difficulties and pressures today, and fueling us to thrive in persecution and crisis in the days ahead.

PRAYER

Jesus, I am moved by the lengths to which You will go and the careful attention You give to my heart and life in Your commitment to bring me forth in mature love and friendship with Yourself. Rather than becoming sidelined or offended when troubles come, I give You my agreement to see every pain, every test, every pressure and every suffering as an invitation into greater intimacy with You. In times of chastening, I trust the One who loves me too much to leave me spiritually poor. Entrusting my times into Your hands, I give You my hope and my love.

STEPS FORWARD IN KEEPING PASSION FOR JESUS

- Bring to the Lord in prayer the past seasons of challenge or difficulty that have left you disillusioned and confused. Willingly offer these to Jesus and ask Him to bring from them the good of deepened intimacy with Himself.

- Talk to the Lord about His chastening in your life. How has it felt? Have you felt harmed or loved? Ask the Holy Spirit to reframe any chastening that has not felt loving so you can behold the Father's heart with revelation and allow future discipline to have its good work in your life.

- Meditate on parts of Scripture that reveal the beauty of Jesus (Psalm 45:1–7; Song of Solomon 5:10–16, Revelation 1:10–17) and realign your heart with Him as your Treasure.

- Consider what it means to have a deep friendship with Jesus. What might that look like for you? What does it include? What does it not include?

Walking in Forgiving and Fervent Love for One Another

t was after I had left town, after I had pulled my deadweight heart away for a few days to seek the Lord in prayer. That weekend was a special weekend for IHOPKC. We had reached the nineteen-year mark of night-and-day prayer. Nineteen years of nonstop worship and intercession, spanning every single 2:00 or 3:00 a.m. hour of any given night, never ceasing since 1999. As a special gift for this anniversary, the Lord sent one thousand Chinese church leaders from across the globe, "converging" at IHOPKC for four days of prayer, worship and fellowship— many of them from the persecuted Church. In the time they were in Kansas City, the Lord began to move among us in a historic way. While I was away, in a matter of days the Holy Spirit began to stir hearts and lives within our spiritual family, healing some of the pain of past seasons.

Several years prior to their coming, the Lord had shifted things among the Chinese by strongly emphasizing the need to build a healthy community—to love one another as family, to be their brother's keeper and to live more intentionally in walking together. This truly was a shift from their previous church culture, yet they responded wholeheartedly to the Lord and changed many things. When they visited IHOPKC, we were direct recipients of this shift.

These breathtakingly Christlike Chinese brothers and sisters—with a love so tangible for us and one another—ministered love and washed the feet of many of our leaders, my friends and peers. But I wasn't there. I was missing this key moment of healing my heart so needed. *Lord, are You kidding me?* I prayed, as I watched the screen of the transpiring service from my hotel room. After a long decade of much corporate difficulty and heartache, another wave of accusation and a sense of exclusion washed over me. *Now? You choose to come like this while I'm away?*

A few days later I came home, and found myself sobbing my pained heart out, unfiltered and raw, in a huddle of surrounding comrades and friends after the Sunday morning service. All the billowing feelings of loss and confusion commingled with a new searing sense of being excluded from a fresh work of God in our spiritual family, the accuser breathing in my ear. And something unexpected happened. Those who had experienced the healing love that came through the tears of our Chinese brothers and sisters now ministered to me in the same way. They hovered around me like a human covering as I wept my heart out in sorrow. They wept with me, prophesied over me and ministered the Lord's heart to me. It was one of the most tender moments of my life. The Lord didn't want me watching only from a distance, but here, with my brothers and sisters, in my vulnerability.

In retrospect, I believe the pain of feeling I had missed out on His work among us was the severe tearing my heart needed in order to go to depths I had never gone in openness, unguardedness and vulnerability with my brothers and sisters in Him. The wounding of my heart necessitated a binding up, but

He wanted that healing to come through the tears, the words and the love of those hovering over me in prayer. The brothers and sisters in Christ who participate in the binding up of our wounds also become bound to our hearts forever. The healing is inextricable from the friends who are part of it. As these surrounding friends let their own hearts bleed with mine, weeping with me, their tears and words extinguished the power of the accusations in my mind and heart. I left the service that day different from when I had arrived. I had walked in to join peers in ministry, but I left with sisters and brothers—ones who bleed together, who cover one another in weakness, who share in joy and sorrow together.

The persecuted believers of the Chinese church modeled a breathtaking humility in their love and brotherly affection for one another. Even as they ministered to our spiritual family, they moved with profound trust for one another, deferring to one another when the Lord seemed to be moving upon different ones, bowing out and making room for another without insecurity, envy or rivalry. When the Lord highlighted one person, the rest would come around in support, celebrating the Lord's hand on that one. They knew one another's strengths and weaknesses and would humbly operate as a body, putting one forward to lead, then another, with a sweet sense of confidence in their love and trust of each other's motives rather than competition and suspicion.

These most noble Chinese men and women taught us that unity of heart arrives through the bloody birth canals of forgiveness and fervent love. It comes through the powerful bond of sharing in both joy and suffering. They told us that when it reached the point that gathering together could mean going to prison, they continued to gather, vowing to go together if that time came; and that love tore open their hearts for one another. Like watching a true demonstration of the weighty love of Jesus poured out among a family, we were marked irrevocably. And as the seeds of their love continue to bear fruit in us, we are still experiencing the impartation and impact.

For me personally, the Lord unfolded an invaluable truth in the wake of our time and experience with our beloved Chinese family: Keeping first love for Jesus is inextricably tied to the brothers and sisters in Christ He has set among us. In my story, the Lord had every intention of restoring and igniting my heart again, but He refused to escort me forward into that full recovery in *isolation*.

In order to have our first love for Jesus not only awakened in us, but *kept* and *preserved* in its full fire, no matter the difficulty in our relationships or the severity of darkness we face in the days ahead, it must be united together with the affection-fires of other believers in Christ. Just as we are members of one another, we are keepers of one another's flame. And we cannot get to the finish line of first love apart from one another.

The Bond between Our Love for Jesus and Our Relationships

About first love for Jesus, the subject of love for one another arises as inseparable to the storyline. Jesus called us not only to love the Lord with all our heart, soul, mind and strength, but to love one another—His second command being much like the first. The two commands are bound up together and cannot be separated because there is an overlapping interdependency within them. On the one side, we only love others to the measure we have personally known and received the love of Christ, and without a deep experience of the love of Jesus, the smallest conflicts will divide us. Living in the first commandment is critical to the fulfillment of the second commandment. On the other side, our relationships with one another, as those redeemed in Jesus, are vital to living victoriously in our love for God and our walk of faith. The Lord has given us this love within His Body as a preserving mechanism to keep our hearts in tenderness and passion, keeping and guarding us from growing hardened and dull. If we neglect these relationships or fall into the snare of offense and bitterness, our relationship with the Lord directly suffers.

I remember when it dawned on me, like one of those truths you wish was wrong even though you know it's right: "Oh no," I sighed, the truth sinking in. It was the moment when I realized my vision to love Jesus with all my heart was at stake. I found myself in a difficult and painful place in one of my friendships. Negative words had been spoken to others about me, casting a shadow over the way they saw me and, in a practical way, hindering my ability to continue in a specific role of ministering that had been a joy to me. The sting of what felt like a sharp rejection tore at and wounded my heart. Instantly, I found myself at a juncture of one of those pivotal moments in life when the easy road is far more enticing than one would have anticipated. I felt the subtle pull toward the path of offense, of putting up a wall of division or whispering defensive words to another friend. But in that moment, I realized how all the paths were connected. If I chose to walk according to the way of accusation or division or even subtle dishonoring of that person, it would have a direct effect not only on that friendship but also on my friendship with Jesus.

Love cooled toward others equals love cooled toward the Lord; they are not separate realties.

Beyond that test and the continual fight for the unoffended heart toward God—even directly tied to it—lies the test and continual fight for the unoffended heart toward those around us. Those words that feel like sharp-edged rocks wound and tear the heart and leave it bitter. The opportunities for disappointment, resentment and offense outnumber the steps of the path, and no one is exempt from their snares. Such adverse relational realities are never neutral.

It is so important that we see the deep connection between our love for Jesus and how we walk out our relationships with one another, so that we might lay hold of the grace the Lord extends to us in these most painful relational conflicts. Our desire to have an open, tender heart that loves Jesus fully is intimately knit to our relationships with others. What we do in relational conflicts holds no small impact on our souls. If we shut our hearts down toward each other, no matter how justified we feel, we ultimately shut down our hearts toward the Lord. If we take the easy road in our relationships—walling off from one another—then over time, we will face the most devastating juncture of all: We will no longer be tender and alive in our hearts toward Jesus.

Our desire to have an open, tender heart that loves Jesus fully is intimately knit to our relationships with others.

Most often, in the middle of these heartaches, we do what comes so naturally for us all: We clamber for a way of escape, a way to self-protect. We defend. We deflect. We self-preserve. Far more apt are we to take the easy and enticing route of self-protection than to pursue that person in love and forgiveness. We are experts at living guarded and hesitant. One little inkling of rejection and we flee for safety by forging a barrier between ourselves and another. We erect interior walls of self-protection in split seconds. We are geniuses at inserting safe distances and space—thinking it wise. And though it is right that we do not entrust our souls and dreams into the hands of others, we must walk carefully in these tests to keep on loving one another and not to shut down our hearts. Self-preservation may make us feel safe, but in the end, it costs us our heart.

Harboring offense in our hearts is the broad and easy path when we feel wounded or mistreated. This course is common in relationships with those in the Body of Christ, because the accuser of the brethren works night and day to divide, steal from and destroy our love and fellowship together. This pattern does not slow down with time, but only increases. The number of years multiplies the number of disappointments, difficulties and seeming justification for offense and bitterness, making the heart that remains tender before God and others one of the rarest finds on earth.

Again, whatever we harbor in our hearts toward our brothers bears a direct result upon our heart-exchange with the Lord. These are not neutral exchanges to the heart, to our love for God and to our future spiritual vitality. Unless we vehemently resist offense and bitterness, and division sowed by the evil one, with a heart resolved to remain tender in love toward our brothers and sisters in Christ, we will sadly wake up one day, wishing our hearts could move in love and worship toward Jesus as they once did, only to find an interior dullness and hardness.

When we see the direct link between our human relationships and our relationship with Jesus, and the potential strike against our passion for Jesus that we might suffer, it causes a holy trembling within us. It forges a tenacity to carefully watch over our hearts—from which flow the wellsprings of life—with all diligence, refusing to allow the thieves and adversaries of love to enter and take root. Compelled by our love for Jesus and desire to remain fervent in Him, we become fiercely committed to love one another, just as the Word of God entreats us. When first loving is in first place and loving the Lord with all our hearts has truly become the dream of our lives, we are empowered to face difficulty and walk out adversity in our relationships. We are endued with the necessary resolve and courage to walk the unpopulated paths of forgiveness and reconciliation with our brothers and sisters.

Bound Together in Christ

Because of this interconnection between our intimacy with Jesus and our bond with one another in Christ, our love for one another finds its source in our personal abiding in the love of Christ; and our own relationship with Jesus is strengthened by our fellowship with one another. In other words, as we grow in intimacy with Jesus, it deepens the way we give ourselves to one another; and as we give ourselves to one another, it impacts and strengthens our relationship with Jesus. We need God to love one another, and we need each other to keep loving and being fervent in God. Thus, when Jesus calls us to love one another as He has loved us, it is not only a call to love each other *in the way* that He loved—laying His life down in servant-hearted, forgiving love—but a call to *receive* the power to love others from Him. It is a call to come to Him in the secret place and receive deep love from Him, and then to extend and give ourselves to one another. He is saying in essence: As you know My love for you more deeply, you will enter a greater grace and gain a broadened capacity to love one another.

The apostle John called loving one another the perfection, or completion, of our love for God. When love abounds and prevails between the members of the Body of Christ, it is a breathtaking work of God, something so extraordinary and other-than, like a crowning and completing divine miracle. This completion cannot happen apart from both God's immeasurable grace poured out to us continually and our persistent resolve to partner with that grace, even during adverse relational conflicts. We are to pursue the bond of peace in every relationship and labor toward the freedom of forgiveness with the forbearing love of Christ. *Here* we find safety from the sin and hardening of heart through unbelief. *Here* we experience an inbreaking of light and joy together in Christ.

Hearts must be torn open before they can heal as one. This is what happens at the cross. We are first torn open over our sin, over our pride, over our ungodliness, and then in turning to Jesus as our only hope of salvation and redemption, we are healed by the only *Balm* that makes well, the only *Person* who can bind up our wounds. Washed in His blood and made new, our story is altogether changed. This place at the foot of the cross is the holy meeting ground that we all stand upon. We have each come individually to its shadow, yet here we are bound together in a new life and new course as members of His Body. From that bloody meeting ground, where our lives were purchased back to God, our pasts washed and our futures rewritten, we are bound forever to those who share in the same rebirth. Together, we are those redeemed by His blood. Together, we are His inheritance.

Individuals are delivered of their individualistic propensities by the power of Christ's shed blood, giving us grace to willingly and courageously draw near to one another in openhearted love and vulnerability. We become bound to one another not only by willpower, or by simply ascribing to right doctrine, but by the revelation of His forgiving love. This God-given understanding and experience of His love empowers us to bleed open in forbearance, forgiveness and openheartedness toward one another, as those standing together upon this meeting ground. Here the love of Christ for us all bridges over our individualistic wakes, forges through every wall, binding our diversity together in tender unity. As brothers and sisters, we freely share in one another's sufferings, willing to face adversity for one another.

Bound together in the forgiving, redeeming love of Jesus and standing as one before the cross, we *vehemently* guard against offenses toward one another. When Jesus calls us to love others as He has loved us, He invites us to forge forward in the grace of the Lord, to cover over offenses, to forgive as He forgave us and to keep the precious bond of peace together. He calls us to *truly love* each other and to keep on forgiving, even seventy times seven times, no matter what offenses we face in our relationships. We are to be bound to one another unbreakably—a bond that holds even when storms come and winds beat upon the house.

This path is far from easy. Though we have need of one another in keeping our fervency in love for Jesus and to strengthen us in warding off the threats to our faith, our *greatest tests* are found in these very relationships. Our greatest relational allies in the good fight of faith are those people positioned most closely to our hearts; yet these relationships also pose the highest threats to our inward spiritual vitality. Is there a more poignant place where pain and potential offense sweep into our hearts and lives than in the context of our relationships with brothers and sisters in Christ? What greater tests are there to the heart than through sin or mistreatment by those we love? Jesus calls us to be radically responsive to His grace when conflicts arise. When mistreatments and disappointments come in our friendships and relationships with those in His Body, pain coloring everything, how we respond and walk these conflicts out together has massive implications on the whole of our lives. So much so that you could say we will only keep our first love for Jesus in as much as we vehemently respond to His grace in the often-turbulent trajectory of loving one another.

Trusting Jesus in the Midst of Our Relationships

Because conflicts in our relationships strike us right to the heart, when we see the connection between our love of one another and our love for God, it can seem impossible to possess a future burning love and passion, both for God and for one another. We question, how will I reach my dream of living with an open heart, tender and not cynical, fervent in first love for Jesus? How does the love of God not get taken out by love of one another?

Yet Jesus does not leave us to ourselves in these times. He alone is our way forward. He is the safe Friend "who sticks closer than a brother" (Proverbs 18:24). He is the perfect One. Our bond of peace between one another is not of our own making. It is only by His blood and by His Spirit dwelling within us, uniting us as His Body. It is a bond bought by holy blood and stretching forth from His forgiving love, just as His outspread arms spanned wide upon the cross. We look not to ourselves but to Him to open our vulnerability, ensure our trust and secure the anchor of our hope.

Desiring to cause our love to increase in fervency rather than decrease, He opens a door of invitation to us wherever we have boarded up our hearts from our brother. With compassion over our guardedness, with tender eyes that search and know, and with a heart that loves and covers, He invites us to open our hearts again. Where we say we can't trust anymore—we've been hurt too many times—He draws near, His eyes appealing for our trust. His very being radiates with the light that reminds us that darkness has not once, from all eternity, been found in Him. *He is the One who can be trusted.* To our folded arms and reticent stance, He walks in the midst of the relationship that brought the barring and opens wide His arms, as though to say, "It's *Me* you must trust here."

The way we keep the second commandment is through the power of the first. We draw from the True Vine, apart from which we can do nothing (John 15:5). We abide in the love that washes and renews and covers. We trust in the faithfulness and perfection not of one another, but of the One who binds us together. Our vulnerable hearts find their safety and confidence in Him, freeing us to generously love one another. We are *all* sure candidates for failing one another, and if we wait for the day of no disappointments, we'll end up shrinking our circles of trusted ones until we have no one left to trust. Our openness toward others and our ability to forgive and trust one another, ultimately, are an openness and trust in *Him*. Without the light of His love, we would still be abiding in death. But because He came and gave His life in forgiving, redeeming love, we have passed from death to life together. In this love, we are bound together. If His love toward us is indestructibly safe, then we can keep our hearts open toward one another and ward off the incremental residues of offense and jadedness that arise.

Trusting Him, we open our hearts and believe all things of others even through disappointments and conflicts—the undergirding being not the faithfulness of each other, but of *Him* and of *His* faithfulness (1 Corinthians 13:7). We receive others not with the guardedness, skepticism and judgmental posture to which we are prone, but in the way Christ received us (Romans 15:7). This is the path forward when we find it difficult to forge ahead together. We place our confidence in the ultimate promise of a transcendent and perfect love that has forgiven us, delivered us, washed us and will never fail. This becomes the freeing vision in the middle of our fallouts and heartaches with others in the Body of Christ.

When we respond to Jesus in these relational testings, the beauty of God will break forth from our broken lives. Though the crises of relationships have the power to ultimately shut down our hearts, even to the Lord, they also have the *potential* to bring us nearer to the heart of Jesus than we've ever been before. When our love runs dry of its original steam, we can witness firsthand the love that never fails, never wearies and never grows faint (1 Corinthians 13:8). When that cycle of self-reliance and self-justification is broken, and when we relinquish the constant fight for self-preservation, we can witness and stand in awe together of the mystery of the love of Christ. We behold the holy love that was lavished upon us—the undeserving and the broken—in all its heights and depths and lengths and widths, surpassing knowledge, yet known by His saints (Ephesians 3:17–19).

As we walk through the invitation to love our brother with hearts open, and all the difficulties that go with it, we refuse the broad road of offense and bitterness. Fighting through the narrowness of longsuffering, believing all things and bearing with one another, we're only at the beginning of the joy of comprehending the love of Christ (1 Corinthians 13:7; Ephesians 3:19; 4:2). We begin to touch what John called the completion of love. In the very places that we imagined we were defeated, because the sorrows were too great and the depth of pain too beyond reconciliation, we find the Lord equipping and giving us every grace not only to *survive* in love, but to *abound* in love.

Fervent, Forbearing Love in the Last Days

Peter spoke of having fervent love for one another in the framework of the end of all things being at hand. In the intensity of that context, he emphasized the necessity of deep devotion to one another (1 Peter 4:7–9). In times of trouble and hostile circumstances, when we are stripped of everything that would have insulated us from the hardship in times past, love is the way forward together. Under pressure and in turmoil, when reserves are low and tensions are high, we are prone to sin toward others more frequently. A multitude of sins arise as well as countless opportunities for offense. And yet Peter spoke of a grace we are given through the cross of Christ that rises to the challenge. It's a love that not only covers a handful of sins, but a multitude. Where sin abounds, grace abounds all the more (Romans 5:20). Where the darkness of our own failures increases, the light of His love shines forth in brightness from our lives and our relationships with one another.

The *fervency* Peter spoke of in our love for others speaks not only of the quality of our sincere affection for each other, but the value we give to our continued fellowship and unity in Him. With fervent zeal, we are to fight to keep the unity of heart and mind, refusing to be divided by the thousand opportunities to draw apart and close off toward each other. Conflicts are inevitable. Misinterpreting one another is unavoidable. Seeing with different perspectives is inescapable. Yet instead of easing into the propensity of separation, we must *fervently* refuse to be divided—whether by explicit discords or by subtle and gradual separations. We carry fervency in our hearts to keep the unity of the fellowship we have together.

This fervent love is our path forward when we face difficulties, yet this path is not always as clear as we imagine it should be. Sometimes we offer forgiveness, but the ones we seek to forgive do not believe they have wronged us. And we find impasses because of differing perspectives or narratives. Again, Paul helps us navigate our way forward even as these impasses increase in times of great pressure and trouble. He does this by distinguishing between forgiving and forbearing, both necessary parts of loving one another. In his letter to the Colossians, Paul spoke of what to do when we find ourselves in relational gridlocks with our brothers and sisters in Christ. In these times, when we feel we have already forgiven but the gridlock remains, He calls us to *forbearance*. As God's chosen ones, holy and beloved, we are to put on tender mercies, kindness, humility, meekness and longsuffering, *bearing with* one another and forgiving one another (Colossians 3:12–14). Paul highlighted a differentiation between forgiveness and forbearance and put them both under the banner of what it means to love one another.

To confess our sins to one another and forgive as Christ has forgiven us—when the barrier between us is resolved through the freedom of forgiveness—this is surely the ideal way forward. But what about the times that we cannot come to the place of seeing a wrongdoing in the same way? When one feels sinned against and the other is sure he did not sin? When the person to whom the offense has been committed would forgive, except that the offender is not asking for forgiveness? They do not think they have done anything wrong. What do we do in these seeming impasses?

In closing a sermon on 1 Peter 4, John Piper helped me see this differentiation that the apostle Paul gave, and it was like the light of understanding to me, revealing an entirely new way forward in loving one another:

> I could wish that in every relationship, church or home, forgiveness would solve all problems. You sin against me, you recognize your sin, [and] call it sin. I forgive you. Restoration. Wonderful. It happens. It ought to happen.
>
> But what if the person sinning against you does not think they are sinning? And you tell them they're sinning, and they're offended? Is the relationship over? Or is there another category? There is another category. It is forbearance. "I will bear you. I will bear with you." Love bears all things, believes all things, hopes all things. What is that, bears all things? It is because we can't get it worked out with forgiveness. We just see things so differently. So you bear with them. That's the only way families and churches survive. So Peter says, "Keep loving one another earnestly because love covers so many things." You just say, "I'll cover it. It's not fixed. Forgiveness would fix it. But it isn't fixed. It is covered."[1]

Forgiveness extended both ways is a healed and fixed relationship, a clean slate. There is grace for this in Christ. Under His cross, as those chosen and holy and beloved to Him, the miraculous happens when two offended hearts can rejoin in unity under the blood in which we've been washed, in Christ. Yet there are also times when we can't seem to be able to work it out together through forgiveness. Our perspectives and narratives on a situation are too different, and we both feel we have the "right" viewpoint. What is the way forward, then? *We forbear.* We bear with one another. We "endure" one another.

We cover over the unfixed relationship with forbearance. Like truth and mercy, forgiveness and forbearance come together and kiss, and a multitude of sins can be covered in their wake.

As troubles increase and the Lord's return draws near, offenses will also increase, and "the love of many will grow cold" (Matthew 24:12). Maligning and mistreatments will multiply. Yet in the very hour when life is harder and sin escalates, something else will increase. Defying the laws of sin and the flesh, *fervent love* for one another will abound in the very heights of increased conflicts and offenses. As stresses surge, both our need for one another and the increase of wrongs done against each other will intensify. In the midst of increased pressure and tensions and trials, we will have more opportunities for offense and more need for forgiveness. More than ever before, we will need to meet together, not neglecting times of gathering, so that we might encourage each other all the more as we see the day of His appearing draw near (Hebrews 10:25). We will not survive without such continual coming together, fervently loving one another in this bond of love, covering a multitude of sins by forgiving and forbearing until the end.

A Love That Never Fails

The love for one another that Jesus invites us into as those in Him is a love that embraces the grace to see above the imperfections of those we love, just as He does. Peter said, "Above all things have fervent love for one another, for 'love will cover a multitude of sins'" (1 Peter 4:8). As believers and those in Christ, our love for one another is to span a multitude of sins like a covering. Our forgiveness for each other, arising from the forgiveness Jesus showed us, is to cover over the wrongdoings between us. Peter spoke of it as loving one another not based on our history or our failures, or even our successes, but on the basis of the *covering love* of Christ.

When we are wronged by someone, we do not make that mistreatment the story of our relationship, relating to that person according to their shortcoming or sin. We do not redefine our relationship now to be about our conflict or difficulty. Rather, our story together and the way we relate to one another, even when we fail each other, is the story of the blood of Jesus' cross and of His forgiving love.

This isn't to say that we gloss over the wrongs done, or that we turn a blind eye to wrongdoing. Such avoidance would be to distort grace rather than to walk in its power. We love in these times not by covering over the sin in the sense of sweeping it "under the carpet." It's not an evading of conflict by ignoring the mistreatment, as though it did not happen. Rather, we are to walk out reconciliation in the way Jesus and the Word of God counsels. We engage in the necessary difficult conversations that we need to have—seeking to live in peace with all (Matthew 18:15–18; Romans 12:18). We work through our grievances together. Yet, when all the conversations have been had, when the mistreatment has been exposed, no matter the wrongdoing, we place everything under the covering of forgiveness, and let it remain there, refusing to dig it up or re-expose it in the future. We view our brother, our sister, primarily according to their relationship to Jesus and only secondarily according to their relationship to us. We consider our relationship with them not according to our conflicts, but according to our *union* in Christ.

This covering, forgiving love is counterintuitive to our flesh but freeing and delivering to our hearts when submitted to by God's grace. Because the pain of mistreatment is so poignant, the most natural response in our flesh is to let that painful offense color every thought we have about that person and alter our every word and action toward them. Yet operating in the opposite spirit is where we will find freedom. We call to mind the glories of who that brother or sister in Christ is before God in their eternal story. We intentionally bless them and thank the Lord for who they are, perhaps even the good things we have shared with them in our history. We bring our thoughts about them and our actions toward them under the story of the love that covers a multitude of sins rather than narrowing our relationship to the offense, mistreatment or misunderstanding we have experienced with them. In this, we avoid the snare of bitterness and hatred, finding freedom in the same forgiveness that set us free from the beginning.

When Paul described to the Corinthian church the love that we are called to offer as those in Christ, He said this love *never fails*. No matter the offense, no matter the mistreatment, no matter the wake of betrayal or wrongdoing, it overcomes. It is a love that forbears, that suffers long, that covers over the gaps and wrongdoings, even as Christ showed forbearing love toward us, suffers long on our behalf and covers over our sins and shortcomings with His blood. The tenderness that He has shown us as individuals, in the way He leads us and the way He washes us with the water of His Word, is the very tenderness we are invited to extend to one another, cherishing each member with loving affection.

I remember coming to a place in a close relationship where I couldn't see the way ahead. The gaps seemed too large. The places of disagreement had stretched too long. Forgiveness felt contrived because it seemed like pretending the rift was resolved. And I went to the Lord in desperation. Surely His Word was true, but I could not see the light of the forward path when all felt obscured in blockades and no-entry points. It was Paul's words in the beloved and often-quoted passage of 1 Corinthians 13 that countered all my conclusions and stood up to my false premise of an impasse too great. *Love never fails* were the three words that stood in my way and lingered in my soul until I submitted to the invincible truth, truer than my feelings, my conclusions or my experiences. Love never fails. And then, like a lighthouse to a ship at sea amid a disorienting and threatening storm, my faith rose to cling to this truth of *unfailing love*, even in the places I had not yet understood. And I wrote with fresh, revived faith:

> Love covers. Where questions linger without answer and old misunderstandings remain cross-armed, love forges ahead with a covering, unthreatened by the gaps beneath (1 Peter 4:8). Love does not wait for the seeing eye-to-eye or the final resolution before it hurries forward to forbear and cover the unsolved and the uncertain (Colossians 3:12–14). Love itself is resolved and certain, needing no perfection in the one it loves in order to advance ahead. Love knows the future even when the present is precarious. It sees the unshadowed day ahead: when broken vessels have been clothed with light and the meek of the earth crowned with glory. In that day, the love that was offered in Christ—before the day dawned and before the shadows fled away—will remain in full brightness (Song of Solomon 4:16; 1 Corinthians 13:13).
>
> The love that I carry for my brother now—though there are gaps and areas we find ourselves unable to resolve—is a love that has only begun its eternal path; and the future is bright. It will remain through the changing of the age, through the ending of the night, and the dawning of the new day. It will not fail but will rush into the days ahead victoriously, covering the broken places and holding together the fault lines, until Love Himself closes them forever.
>
> Love never fails.
>
> And where my words fail, though I may have the tongue of angels, love is greater than all that language can offer. And where prophecy and understanding and even faith seek to bring the light but still come up short, love does not fail, shining brighter and brighter until the perfect day. Where even the highest sacrifice of self-giving cannot reconcile, love lays itself down for another and does not fall short in its offering (1 Corinthians 13:1–3).
>
> Love never fails.

And there is a place—a place where love waits in delay—forging a covering until the shadows flee away. At times it does not know whether the resolutions will come before the day breaks or afterward; but love does not hesitate in that unknowing. It covers. Covers the gaps of misunderstanding. Shields the unresolved from the exposure of the accuser, of the storms, of the threats. It lays itself down over the wounds, over the sins, over the losses and the grief (1 Corinthians 13:4).

If we watch the way of the love of Christ in our relationships with one another, we will surely see. Wherever love is yielded to, it creates a way. Even when words have failed to find resolve and understanding has fallen short to bring the light of agreement, even where sacrifice is insufficient to close the wounds, love presses forward in courage and confidence, covering and forbearing, hoping and believing. It suffers long (1 Corinthians 13:7). It reaches into the sweetness of holy fellowship with Christ and extends itself with open arms just as He opened His arms and gave His life for love (John 13:34).

Whether we find the place where all that was lost is found, and all that was wounded is bound—or whether that day doesn't come until the next age—love never fails.

And love never fails.

When the accuser of the brethren comes and says, "But what of the wrong done? What of the mistreatment unrepented for?" love says, "I'm laying myself down like a covering over the places between me and my brother. I'm not sure when or how we'll fully find one another in reconciliation, but I'm not afraid to hope and believe and lay myself down in forbearance in the delay. Because this I know: Whether we find the place where all that was lost is found, and all that was wounded is bound—or whether that day doesn't come until the next age—love never fails."

Love is the greatest, and it remains. It carries over from age to age. It forges forward and fails not, even through the transition of this life. It is as strong as death and as unyielding as the grave. It triumphs. It overcomes. It transcends even the barrier of death. Many waters cannot quench it, and floods cannot drown it (Song of Solomon 8:6–7; Romans 8:38).

Love never fails.

PRAYER

Jesus, I desire to possess and extend forgiving love to those by whom I have been wronged or those who have injured my heart. I ask for Your grace to drink of, and be tenderized by, Your extravagant love for me—enabling me to overflow in that love and forgiveness for those who have wronged me.

STEPS FORWARD IN KEEPING PASSION FOR JESUS

- What have you been carrying around in your heart that you know you need to give to Jesus? Keeping passion for Jesus is bound to walking in forgiving and fervent love with one another, and thus, to move forward in fiery love, you must offer to the Lord your relationships and forgive where needed.
- Take inventory of things you want to bring before the Lord. Write them down, and systematically work through them with the Holy Spirit, forgiving and asking Jesus for His love for each person and situation.
- Tell the Lord that you believe His love never fails; commit your trust to Him as you seek to walk the way of love through relational difficulties.

Overcoming the Trouble of Accusation and Betrayal

It was the night of the Last Supper, and emotions were high as Jesus expressed the news that one of them would betray Him, leaving the disciples in visible shock and turmoil. You could almost feel the tension in the room as they each looked around, not knowing who it was that Jesus spoke of—each one not knowing if by some terrible turn of events *he himself* had betrayal of Jesus hiding deep within his heart. "Surely not I, Lord?" they began to choke out, one by one. After Jesus revealed this looming crisis, He was troubled in spirit. John leaned back against Him and asked, "Lord, who is it?" Probably in just a whisper, Jesus disclosed to John, "It is he to whom I will give this morsel of bread when I have dipped it." Then, after Judas took the bread, Satan entered him, and Jesus told him, "What you are going to do, do quickly" (John 13:21–38).

You can almost hear the poignant strain in the Good Shepherd's voice. Judas was His friend. He was one of the disciples who had walked with Him for three years (Matthew 26:50).

There was pain in His heart over this, and He did not hide it from the friends surrounding Him.

Jesus was about to endure incredible suffering of many kinds that night, but the heartache of Judas's betrayal was the only pain He voiced aloud. Judas had witnessed so many wonders. He'd gone through so much with Jesus. There was history and shared life and friendship. Though Jesus had purposefully chosen Judas and knew he would betray Him, He still had anguish in His heart in this treachery, also feeling the pain over what was about to unfold in Judas's own life.

That night, Jesus would know both betrayal and denial by his closest friends. How He responded to those who betrayed and failed Him is like a light to us, helping us to know the way forward as we ourselves walk through our own betrayal-soaked pathways. We do not walk alone. Jesus' pain over Judas's betrayal assures us that He fully knows and understands the unusual grief and heartache we experience in these relational crises. And the way He responded to Judas with genuine friendship in the very moment of betrayal shines like a beacon of light to us, modeling how we must respond when we face betrayals in our own lives.

The most perfect Man suffered the most unjust betrayal of all time, and He went to the cross unoffended. He died with a heart free from animosity or dark emotions toward both those who betrayed Him and those who failed Him. This is the One whom we follow, and as we carry in our hearts the betrayals we face in the same way He did—responding as He did in a tender spirit opposite to those who betray us—we will experience not only the same resplendent freedom from offense—shining like the beautiful Lamb shines—but also the even greater miracle, as well: We will possess the freedom and magnanimity of heart to view our betrayers not according to the narrow lens of the set of circumstances or sins, but according to the generous and kind perspectives of God over him or her. We will see them as God sees them, carry the same forgiving and longsuffering heart that He Himself carried when, in His hour of suffering, He prayed, "Father, forgive them. . . ."

A Promise of Mature Love

Only a few hours after they shared the Last Supper together, and after Jesus had told them of the betrayal at hand, knowing and carrying all these tensions in His heart, Jesus prayed for something profound, something beyond our comprehension, something ungraspable to us if taken at face value. It would seem to us almost too lofty to even hope for, especially in the turbulent night and context when these words were spoken, if not for the fact of *who* uttered the words. These are the very prayers of God Himself, the One who took on flesh and possesses the fullness of the Godhead in His frame. The desires and prayers He expressed were the actual groans of the infinite, omnipotent, and sovereign God—the Creator and Sustainer and Redeemer of all. The God-Man, the beloved Son, does not pray *wishful* prayers, but the sure and certain purposes and plans of God. Surrounded by His friends, the young and fearful disciples huddled together before the darkness that the following days would unleash, He lifted His voice and prayed:

> "That they all may be one as You, Father, are in Me, and I in You; that they also may be one in Us, that the world may believe that You sent Me. And the glory which You gave Me I have given them, that they may be one just as We are one: I in them, and You in Me; that they may be made perfect in one, and that the world may know that You have sent Me, and have loved them as You have loved Me. Father, I desire that they also whom You gave Me may be with Me where I am, that they may behold My glory which You have given Me; for You loved Me before the foundation of the world. . . . And I have declared to them Your

157

name, and will declare it, that the love with which You loved Me may be in them, and I in them."

John 17:21–26

We often dismiss New Testament truths as lofty language devoid of actual fulfillment, but if we pause and consider the words of this prayer, and who it was that prayed them, coupled with the dim lights and foreboding context into which these words were spoken that night, we'll find ourselves overwhelmed by the *factual future* into which God is leading His people. Jesus cried out that we would be *one* as the Father is in the Son and the Son in the Father, that we would be one in Them. For this purpose of being made perfect in oneness together in Him, He gave us the glory that the Father gave Him. That the world would know and behold something so other-than, so stupefying, so transcendent and divine, that they would know that God sent His Son. He prayed that the very love with which the Father loved the Son—that holy and inexhaustible flame of love—would be in us, and He in us. And these prayers He spoke into the dark night air, heavy with imminent betrayal, failures and denial by all the shaking hearts circled around Him.

These are important tensions to carry because we might either believe the lofty words to be true, but extract them from their context, leaving us unprepared for the adversaries ahead; or we might see only the circumstances of betrayal and failure and broken humanity and dismiss these promises as impossible—hyperbole at best, and misleading overstatement at worst. Yet, keeping the backdrop of that dark night before our understanding and then hearing these prayers of the God-Man, who, even facing His own suffering, did not back down from their promise, we are filled with faith to believe that no obstacle is too great—whether betrayals by loved ones or our own persecution—to stand in the way of these sure and sovereign purposes of God for His Church.

In the prayer of Jesus that He lifted to His Father that night, we behold and hear His everlasting desire and plan to cause us to know and comprehend and experience, individually and together, the love of God in Christ. He refuses to relent until we burn in love for Him and possess abounding, fervent, self-giving love for one another. A love that defies and overcomes the trajectory of fear and accusation and division. A love that lays down its life for others in joyful givenness. A love that is tender, authentic, sincere and from the heart. A love so transcendent and other-than in its nature that it causes all to know we are His disciples, that it compels the world to know that the Father sent the Son and has *loved us* as He loved His Son. He is committed to maturing us into this Gospel light of divine love.

We cannot look ahead with rightful expectation unless we peer into the very heart cries of the Son of God with full expectancy of their glorious realization. These words of Jesus are before us as a prophetic witness, like light breaking forth amid a darkened sky. The future that He is leading the family of God to, as we partner with His grace, is so beautiful, so overwhelming, that it will leave us undone and cut to the heart by God's breathtaking kindness and tenderness. We will marvel with wonder at His extraordinary ability to bring forth the weak ones of the earth—broken and fractured as we are—as bright and shining ones who reflect and display the very love and goodness of God to the earth (John 13:35; 17:23).

> **We cannot look ahead with rightful expectation unless we peer into the very heart cries of the Son of God with full expectancy of their glorious realization.**

Yet how will He do it? How will we, as brothers and sisters in the Body of Christ, get there? How do we move from where we are, in all the divisions and factions and offenses and judgments and enmity we have, to this profound, miraculous place of unity that Jesus prayed for in His high-priestly prayer? How will we love as He loves and forgive as He forgives? How will we extend longsuffering and patient love to one another in the places we've been most severely divided and fractured? How will we not only overcome accusation and division, but come forth victorious in a miraculous, fervent love for one another? How will we embrace this blood-stained cross called forgiving love and live without bitterness, wrath, anger, clamor and evil speaking—but rather, with kindness and tenderheartedness toward one another (Ephesians 4:31–32)?

These questions, and the problem of the gap between what we presently know and what the Word of God promises lies ahead for those in Christ, bring us to face the unavoidable subject of *accusation and betrayal* among the family of God. We have layers of unbelief related to the miraculous future that Jesus prayed for because we have known the adversaries of love and the pain of injured and severed relationships in the Body of Christ. Even if we have not known the full bitterness of outright betrayal, we've known shadows of accusation, division, distance and doubt. Not only do our hearts need healing from these relational fractures—past and present—but we need Jesus to gently expose and uproot any dormant seeds of betrayal hiding within our own hearts. Like the disciples, we need to ask the question, "Is it I?" and allow Him to search us and see if there is any wicked way in us, leading us forward in the way everlasting (Psalm 139:24).

First, He wants to elevate our vision of the certain future of the Body of Christ's inheritance of living caught up together in God's own love—in the ever-burning fellowship and delight of the Trinity—convincing us of the *possibility* and *certainty* of the miraculous transformation in His people and delivering us from all unbelief related to that future. *Then*, He wants to show us the way forward—the paths that lead us from broken relationships and broken hearts, with histories of the pain of betrayal, and guide us to the love that abounds still more and more, glorifying God with one heart and one mind, the good and pleasing unity of brothers, bound in holy, forgiving love, reconciled together and one in Him (Psalm 133:1; Romans 15:6; Philippians 1:9).

Our Destiny: A Love That Overcomes Accusation and Betrayal

The miracle that Jesus is bringing forth in His people at the end of the age is the splendid transformation of the global Body of Christ into a *radiant Church* (Ephesians 5:27). This radiance lies in the perfection of her love and the fulfillment of both the first *and* the second commandments. We together will possess the qualities of *first love* all the way to the end, with loyal love to Jesus, fervent love for one another and overcoming love for our enemies. We will possess and impart a love that covers over a multitude of sins and is gentle and kind with accusers. We will be bound together—a corporate people made up of those from every tongue and tribe and nation, every differing stream and kind—having overcome the schemes of accusation and fear, devised by the accuser of the brethren, with the very love of God, the love that many waters cannot quench (Song of Solomon 8:6–7; John 17:24–26; Revelation 12:10–11).

The Church will come into this radiant destiny and miraculous love not by conditions becoming easier, but in the context of the darkest hour of human history. As His return draws near, the love that will come forth from His people will arise from the fiercest betrayal and environment of accusation in human history (Matthew 5:44; 10:21; 24:7–10). We have already begun to see the beginnings of this hostile environment emerging in our day, but it will only increase as His return draws near. Paul described that time as when men will be lovers of themselves rather than lovers of God, and Jesus spoke of the hearts of many growing cold in the wake of the offenses and betrayals that would mount up in that context (Matthew 24.12, 2 Timothy 3:1–5). Yet amid this most adverse relational backdrop of all time, where brother is betraying brother and children are turning against their parents, a bright and shining light will break forth from the family of God. From the most hate-filled and love-grown-cold atmosphere will simultaneously arise an awe-inspiring, longsuffering love from God's people, a love that is gentle as God is gentle, patient as God is patient, longsuffering as God is longsuffering. A love that has triumphed over the divisions and enmity sown by the accuser of the brethren (John 17:20–26).

The openhearted, tender, and unoffendable love that God is bringing forth in His sons and daughters must be strong enough to face and overcome the fiercest and most poignant opponents of love—arising in the most hostile circumstances. Again, only the undiluted love of God Himself, imparted by His Spirit and received and experienced by us—utterly transforming us—will be sufficient to withstand the darkness of that hour. Jesus will bring together the most inconceivable reconciliations. Enemies will be united as dear friends. Differing streams in the Body of Christ will champion one another with a sincere love that knows its need of the other. Racial and social tensions and divides will be healed by the love and blood of Christ, not only in word, but in actuality. Brothers and sisters, mothers and fathers, friends will have so known and experienced the tender gentleness, goodness, and love of Christ that they will possess the grace to forgo fleshly desires and propensities to defend themselves or accuse others, whether out of bitter jealousy or selfish ambition. Instead, they will overflow with the love and tender delight that they have known in Jesus, imparting that same love to one another (John 15:12; James 3:16–17).

Even beyond forgiving and blessing our enemies, Jesus wants to bring His Church to the miraculous place of seeing the brothers and sisters who most mistreat us as *He sees them*, feeling for them *as He feels*, and saying over them *what He says*. He wants to so transform our interior by the depths of His extravagant grace and love—the love that laid down its life for its enemies—that we begin to emulate our Father, as sons of God who reflect Him, in our responses to those who betray us (Matthew 5:44).

Rather than giving way to the offense and accusation sweeping the culture and generation, we will enter God's own generous perspective and narrative over His people. God does not see as man sees. He does not look at the outward, but at the heart (1 Samuel 16:7). We often see brothers and sisters in the Body of Christ through the narrow lens of their weakness or failure, reducing people to their deficiencies, but God sees and receives them through the wide lens of their comprehensive, eternal beauty before Him.

He sees the secret motives of the heart, the sincere reaches toward Him, and the prayers prayed to Him that no other knows about, hidden from the eyes of men. He sees His sovereign calling on their lives. He sees those in the Body who are mistreating or betraying us not with the narrow, myopic lens through which we are prone to view them—fixating only on the actions that are presently hurting us. Rather, He beholds them through the unspeakably lavish and broad lens of their eternal identity. He beholds not only a fraction of their lives, but the entirety. He sees all the good and noble things about them that we either dismiss or cannot perceive, because they are the hidden virtues and motives of the heart, and He evaluates them according to that narrative.

The most rare and astounding love in all human history is the love that views our brother in the way that God has viewed us, feels for our sister in the way that God feels for us and speaks of one another in the way that He speaks over us.

This is a love that reaches across the divides of betrayal as a covering and binding bridge, refusing the separation. Rather than reducing our friends to the facts of their accomplishments and deficiencies, this way of evaluating one another makes room for the broad and generous story that the Lord writes over the lives of those persons, according to His extravagant mercy and grace.

As impossible as it can sometimes seem, the Lord invites us into the confident believing that this is in fact our future together. Extraordinary and precious in its rarity, Jesus will mature this holy and tender love in His Church at the end of the age. She will come forth refined by the leadership of Jesus that allowed the betrayals and persecutions to yield His triumphant love. She will be radiant with a miraculous, forgiving love that extends and lays itself like a covering across seemingly insurmountable fractures and betrayals and treachery. Her love for one another and for her enemies will cover over breaches and divides with breathtaking perseverance and joy. Defying the brokenness and sin of man, her love—which is God's own love—will triumph where every self-strengthened willpower could not muster. The Bride of Christ will possess the very same love for one another by which she herself has been loved in Christ Jesus—the tender and cherishing love that washes with the water of the Word, continually holding in view the glorious radiant future Jesus is leading us into together (Ephesians 5:25–30).

The Paths of Abounding Love

We have considered the glorious destiny the Lord is bringing His Church into, our vision elevated to behold with faith—and refuse unbelief—that He will, in fact, bring us there. Yet, what does this look like in our day-to-day lives? What is the path that will lead us into this mature and miraculous love? Though it would seem almost too simplistic, the way forward is found in Jesus' Sermon on the Mount, when He said:

> But I say to you, love your enemies, bless those who curse you, do good to those who hate you, and pray for those who spitefully use you and persecute you, that you may be sons of your Father in heaven. . . . Therefore you shall be perfect, just as your Father in heaven is perfect.
>
> Matthew 5:44–45, 48

As familiar as we are with these words of Jesus, they hold the lamp that enlightens our darkness in the heartache of betrayal—the most painful wound to the heart. We often fail to recognize that, when Jesus spoke of *enemies*, He was alluding not only to strangers, but to friends or family members to whom we are very close. They are the ones who have become an enemy through a relational conflict. This is why the pain is most poignant. The bitter cup that Jesus drank as He went to the cross and suffered and died—the most agonizing and wounding to His heart—was surely the betrayal by close friends. There is nothing that cuts and pains the heart more deeply.

Betrayal by a friend or family member stands in its own category of pain and heartache. It wounds more profoundly than most every pain known to the human heart because it happens not with strangers, but with those close to us. A betrayal usually arises out of a deeply rooted offense or a sense of mistreatment in the heart of the one betraying us, and compounding the complexity of this, we do not usually see it coming, leaving us unprepared, with hearts unguarded, when it strikes. David professed:

> For it is not an enemy who taunts me—then I could bear it; it is not an adversary who deals insolently with me—then I could hide from him. But it is you, a man, my equal, my companion,

my familiar friend. We used to take sweet counsel together;
within God's house we walked in the throng.

Psalm 55.12–14 ESV

The Man of Sorrows knew the most bitter betrayals by close friends, more than any man in human history, and yet from that place of rejection and being despised, He cried out that the Father forgive them. He revealed to us how even these virulent gridlocks of betrayal and hostility do not bar the love of God in Christ. They are not more powerful than the love that many waters cannot quench (Song of Solomon 8:6–7). If we will yield to Him in these relationships, by drinking the cup that He drank and submitting to His path of longsuffering love—hoping all things, believing all things and forbearing with our brethren—we will find the miraculous nature of Christ's love to prove true. *It never fails.* It finds a way. It forges a path, overcomes the obstacles and defeats the adversaries.

We will never reach the finish line of the first commandment—of keeping first love all our days, of maturing in love so fully that we stand unoffended, holy and blameless before Him—unless we possess understanding of how to walk through the pain of accusation and betrayal in God's prescribed way, developing a history with Him in these trials, no matter the frequency or the degree that they cross our path. When we experience such severed relationships and torn trust as David described, we suffer the blow that could very well take us out if we do not actively engage with Jesus in pressing forward in love.

The only way to the glorious miracle of *complete unity*, as Jesus prayed for, is by embracing and imparting Jesus' counsel in Matthew 5:44—to love, bless, pray for and do good for those who mistreat, persecute and betray us. We must actively engage with the Lord's heart over them, refusing the narrative of the accuser, or even our own limited evaluations of them. Fighting to possess the Lord's mind and carry His heart will be our way forward and the key to overcoming these relational divides and fractures. Satan's great weapon against God's people is his twofold accusation against them—to convince them to accuse themselves, and then to accuse one another. Only by overcoming this accusation can God's people walk with confidence before Him and in mature love for each other (John 17:23).

We need God's perspective over our brother who has mistreated us. We need the mind of Christ over our friend who has accused us. And gaining God's perspective takes time and requires labor in the soul. To enter the viewpoint that God holds, seeing them as God sees them, does not happen instantly, but over time, as we actively engage in praying, blessing and doing good for them.

To see myself as God sees me is difficult enough, let alone someone who has betrayed me—especially when that person is someone with whom I have labored, someone in my family or someone to whom I've been close. Yet the Lord invites us to call to remembrance again how He has forgiven us, how He has shown us great kindness and love in our weaknesses and deficiencies, and then to view that person with the same lens. He beckons us into the constant abiding in His own love, and to draw upon that perfect fellowship and deep affection as our power source in moving forward into this triumphant love.

David showed us the way forward in contending against this accusation when he said His "gentleness has made me great" (Psalm 18:35). Speaking of the way God loves and evaluates, David declared how God's gentleness with him in his weaknesses and deficiencies was the very pathway to his greatness. As David received and experienced the gentleness of God toward him, he became equipped to impart that same gracious gentleness to others, even his enemies. This was what made David *great* before God, a man after God's own heart. He related to others in the way God related to him. When he encountered the weakness and deficiency of others, David responded to them in the way God responded to his own shortcomings—with extravagant gentleness. This pathway is the way to true greatness.

As we voluntarily labor in our souls to see as Christ sees and love as He loves, our souls are brought back into the remembrance of the grace that saved and redeemed us. Our hearts are washed and renewed as we recall the abundance of His gentleness and lovingkindness. This equips us to *impart* the same grace and gentleness to those who have wronged us. We become transformed within and made ready to express the goodness and gentleness of God to others, even those close relationships that have caused us the greatest pain and adversity (Psalm 18:5; Matthew 5:44–45).

> There's something so specifically refining and life-changing to the soul when we actively love and bless those in the family of God who accuse or betray us.

There's something so specifically refining and life-changing to the soul when we actively love and bless those in the family of God who accuse us or betray us. Laying hold of the grace Jesus extends to us in this holy pursuit, as difficult as it is, produces something transcendent in us. The drinking of this cup—the cup of forgiving and blessing and praying for those who mistreat and persecute us—is only made possible through our fellowship with Jesus, abiding in His love and drinking of the consolation of His Spirit. Yet when we walk it out in our relationships, it liberates our souls. Rather than remaining locked toward these, we are washed with Jesus' perspective and emotions over them, freeing us to share in that viewpoint and feeling. Our hearts are freed to experience the affections He possesses and love them as He loves them.

This liberty to love is what will cause the world to look on with wonder and proclaim, "Look at how they love one another!" This is the maturity in love that Jesus is leading us to and that He cried out for in His high-priestly prayer. There is coming a day when even the highest intercessory cries of the God-Man Himself will come forth in stunning fulfillment. The very love with which the Father loved the Son will burn like fire within us, shining forth from our lives and making us one as the Father and Son are one (John 17:21–26). The miraculous future of the Body of Christ—*our future*—is a unity that is forged through the fires of forgiveness and a oneness that overcomes all the assaults of the accuser of the brethren (Revelation 12:11).

Love Is Beautiful, but Not Clean

These are easy truths to talk about and gleaming promises to speak of, yet when the pain of close relationships turned adversarial weighs heavy upon the heart, these are messy, heart-rending realities to walk out. Navigating through them, as simple as the path is that Jesus gave us, can be anything but smooth.

I remember the pain in my own heart over such a breach in a close friendship, and the churning confusion and grief that went along with it. Amid that heartbreak, knowing in my head what Jesus said of how to walk these things out, I still felt like I was walking around with a torn limb, bleeding out. There was nothing straightforward or composed about any of it. Yet Jesus doesn't ask us to walk alone in these times. He doesn't give us the path forward and then send us on our way. He is always right beside us. He is beneath these crosses of love with us, showing us the way. In that time, when the surprise of love's heartache left me questioning if maybe I had even let love take me too far in its wrestle and heartache, the Lord showed me a glimmering piece of beauty amidst disheveled shards of heart: This is *how loving one another looks at times*—though messy and painful, it does not diminish its beauty. Or its genuineness as real love. *Love suffers* long. In that time, I wrote:

> Love is beautiful, but it's not clean. It frees the heart from unforgiveness and bitterness, while not even slightly delivering it from pain and heartache. Freedom of forgiving love does not mean living scot-free and untouched. Love is mangled and wounded and messy, or it has not even begun its race.
>
> Love is a bloody cross and a disfigured Body. Love is beautiful, but it's not clean. It's not off the hook and fancy-free. It feels the pain at every turn. It tears with the divides at every movement. When we feel pain and mourn over the rifts, it is not an indication of our hearts having submitted to another's hold over our soul, but rather, love doing what it does. It suffers long, sometimes to agonizing measures.
>
> Love will never get to the end of its battle in one piece. Free of offense, yes. Uncontrolled by accusation and bitter anger, yes. Delivered from self-seeking envy and the like—yes. But not free of sorrow. Not free of bleeding-hearted intercession and mourning. Not free of messy groans and tears that refuse to be dried in the middle of its long battle. Tears and groans born out of the conviction that there is always yet hope.
>
> Pain and heartache are not red flags to love—just the usual, standard markers along the path. Burning stabs of grief and distress are not indicators of areas unsubmitted to Jesus, or places given over to the control of another's hold. Rather, these pangs are just part of the bloody path of forgiving love—the path where no one shows up to the end unscathed. These achings are common companions to the ones living under the lordship of the bleeding King who is the Lamb of God.
>
> Love is not controlled and composed, but bleeding, desperate believing in the face of every tight-fisted opposition. It beats the ground and refuses to receive the cold diagnosis

claiming its efforts are in vain, that the dire prognosis is inevitable. Love is beautiful, but it's not clean.

As Andrew Peterson painted the picture so poignantly: "It'll wake you up in the middle of the night, it'll take just a little too much. It'll burn you like a cinder till you're tender to the touch. It'll chase you down, and swallow you whole, it'll make your blood run hot and cold. Like a thief in the night, it'll steal your soul, and that's a good thing. Love is a good thing."[1]

Love is free of fear, but it's anything but free of pain. It is free of self-seeking, but it's anything but free of desperate pounding upon the door in prayer. It is no foreigner to aching and weeping and mourning, even when the war is long and the victory bleak. It won't relent. It won't pull out. It refuses to sit on the sidelines from a safe distance but inserts itself in the middle of the disarray. It clings to the promise of the blood that triumphed and the wounds that healed. The blood that continues to wash and forge through barriers and cover over sin's multitude of offenses. The longest of paths are the bloodiest of victories. And love never knew a triumph without a blood-stained cross and piercing thorns accompanying its way. Love is beautiful, but it's not clean.

The love that Jesus is bringing forth in His Church, burning and shining, is the same cross-bearing love that He Himself possesses, puts on display and imparts to our hearts. With the same cherishing, nourishing love with which He has loved us as individuals, we are in turn to love one another in the Body of Christ. This is not easy—in fact, it is spiritually violent. To take up our cross and love in this way is as dying with the Lord. Yet this is love. And it is with this Lamb of God–like love that His Church will arise at the end of the age. It will take all our strength and perseverance to enter by the grace of God, but we will be awestruck when it emerges. We will love as He loves. We will shine as He shines.

Imparting the Love of Our Crucified Bridegroom

Once again, as miraculous and glorious as the Church's destiny is, the pathway can feel daunting and insurmountable. The instruction to love as He loved can sit bland in our mouths with our incapacity to process and engage with Him in it. How do we move into this ability to possess and impart the love of Christ, reflecting the love of our Father, as sons and daughters who look like Him? Again, it is the revelation of the Bridegroom and His self-giving love for us that matures *our* love, even our love for one another. When we are mistreated or betrayed, or when we find ourselves in a devastating breach of relationship, if we will labor in our souls to purposefully take that offense before the foot of the crucified Bridegroom's cross, it will change our hearts toward our brother or sister in Christ.

As we call to mind how our Beloved Jesus loved us and washed us from our sins, even while we were living in our harlotry, we are washed with the comfort and consolation needed to disarm the accusations of the enemy—both toward ourselves and toward one another. When we are washed by His Word and tenderized by His cherishing love that is the very agent of our maturity, our hearts are softened toward one another, as those joined together in Him. Our hearts are transformed from hearts of stone to hearts of flesh, overflowing with that *same love* to the brother or sister who has mistreated or betrayed us. With the same love that we encounter in His heart as the Bridegroom toward us—cherishing and delighting in us—we are empowered to love one another.

The very delight that transformed us, and continues to wash and renew us, is the key to unlocking our hearts toward those by whom we are wounded. The accusations lose their power in the wake of Christ's overwhelming love. The sense of mistreatment loses its power in the wake of being loved so excessively, though we were entirely undeserving. I go back to His delight in me, though I am the unworthy one, and it tenderizes my heart toward the one I am seeking to love with a forgiving, overcoming love.

Our eyes become washed in the way we behold one another, seeing each other through the eyes of Christ, in the narrative He holds—a perspective saturated with divine gentleness and generosity. How can we be divided if He is not divided (1 Corinthians 1:13)? How can we slander one another if this is not the way He speaks to us? How can we compete and strive against one another when we are, in fact, members of one another, united in Him; and not only belonging to Him, but belonging to one another (Ephesians 4:25)?

We are caught up together in the greater storyline in which we mutually share. We are escorted into the marvelous narrative that He possesses over everyone's life—each one indispensable to the whole—rather than remaining in our own skewed and reductionist evaluations of ourselves and others. Through this exchange—as we trade our own narrow perspective for Jesus' view—our hearts are tenderized to feel what He feels toward our brethren and love others as He loves them.

The very love that won us over, that tenderized and awakened our affections, that evoked our deepest desires and quenched our deepest longings—can we turn and give that same love to our brother? To our spouse? To our children? What of the one who has betrayed us? What of those who were friends but became our enemies? Can we pray for them and bless them in our hearts with the same loving and generous love by which we have been transformed? Can we draw from the comforts that we have found in His tender affections and offer that same tenderness to them, knowing that the One who is so moved by our weak love is also moved by our brother in Christ who has wounded us? That the One who is so patient with our stumbling forward is also long-suffering with our friend who betrayed us? That the Bridegroom who is ravished over us is also ravished over them

(Song of Solomon 4:9)? Can we behold how we together are the saints who make up the riches of the glory of His beautiful inheritance, promised to Him by His Father and purchased by His holy blood?

Taking the sweetness of His love for us, that consolation of His delight in us, that tenderness of heart He has produced in us, we turn to the relational conflict we are walking through with our brother, and we apply that same tender affection to him. We engage with Jesus this way in prayer, asking for His heart and blessing our brother, lifting him before God in intercession. Transformation occurs in our souls even when our prayers feel feeble and laborious. Responding to Jesus, we pray and bless and do good for them, and our emotions change over time. We pray, "Jesus, You delight in him. He moves Your heart, even as I move Your heart. He is so dear to You. Jesus, let me see him as You see him and feel for him as You feel for him. Let me possess Your heart, Your delight, Your emotions and Your evaluation of him."

Possessing interior lives transformed by His delight and enjoyment, we will have the courage and consolation to overflow with the same generous, gentle, forgiving love to one another, even to unbelievers. The world will behold a light of love arising from the broken lives of God's people, our love looking like His and culminating as His did, as an inbreaking brightness: *the light of the world* (Matthew 5:14–16). And we ourselves will know we have indeed "passed from death to life" because we love one another (1 John 3:14).

Dwelling together as brethren in unity, having loved one another with the same generous, long-suffering, tender love with which God has loved us, we will "walk in the light as He is in the light," having "fellowship with one another" (Psalm 133:1; 1 John 1:7). The very love with which the Father loved the Son, loyal and long and deep, will be the coursing power filling our hearts and minds and radiating through our works and actions.

The true light of His love—that which is true in Him and in us—will shine forth increasingly "until the day dawns and the morning star rises" (2 Peter 1:19).

PRAYER

Jesus, You know the pain and the heartache of betrayal. You are with me in the most poignant sorrow. I ask for the miraculous grace that You impart to the human heart: not only to forgive as Christ has forgiven me, but also to see the one who I feel betrayed me not in the narrow lens of their deficiency, but according to the grand story of how You see them. Let me see as You see, feel as You feel and say what You say over them.

STEPS FORWARD IN KEEPING PASSION FOR JESUS

- Turn your attention to the promise of Scripture and of Jesus' high-priestly prayer found in John 17. Allow your heart to be stirred and your faith renewed by the future Jesus wants to bring us into together as His Church.
- Commit to Him every relationship where you have known betrayal, and after forgiving and committing that relationship to the Lord, cry out in prayer to enter the very heart of Jesus over them—that you would begin to taste of His miraculous love.

Laying Hold of the Promise of Light, Love and Joy Together

The year was 1988, and on a hot July day, the 33-year-old pastor, Mike Bickle, found himself in his office, rummaging through mail and stumbling upon a wedding card with a Bible verse that caught his eye:

> Put me like a seal over your heart, like a seal on your arm. For love is as strong as death, jealousy is as severe as Sheol; its flashes are flashes of fire, the very flame of the LORD. Many waters cannot quench love, nor will rivers overflow it; if a man were to give all the riches of his house for love, it would be utterly despised.
>
> Song of Solomon 8:6–7 NASB1995

Something stirred in Mike's heart as he read these words, and he understood this to be the invitation of Jesus to His Church, His Bride. His heart instantly caught up in prayer, Mike began to join the prayer of Jesus from John 17 together with these words in Song of Solomon: "Jesus, seal my heart with Your fiery love. You, Yourself, be the seal upon my heart. Father, keep Your promise to Your Son by causing me to love Him like You do. Let that very love be in me. Let my heart burn with this seal of fire, this everlasting flame of Your love."

As Mike prayed, the presence of the Holy Spirit began to rest on him in a unique way. He began to weep gently, and he felt such a tenderizing in his heart by the Lord that he called his receptionist and asked not to be interrupted by any phone calls for a while. He wanted to continue in this precious and powerful time with the Lord.

The tenderizing of the Spirit increased as he wept before the Lord. He continued praying, "Jesus, I want more of this love for You that is stronger than death."

Only a few minutes later, his phone rang—the very thing he had asked not to happen! Confused, and a bit bothered by the unwelcome interruption, he answered the phone. The apologetic voice of his receptionist explained that Bob Jones (a prophetic man who was a part of Mike's ministry at the time) was on the line and he said he had just heard the audible voice of the Lord for Mike. Of course, Mike understood and agreed that he wanted to take this call.

Bob was late to catch a flight, and his words, thick with Arkansas drawl, tumbled out hurriedly: "Mike, I only have a minute. I've just heard the audible voice of the Lord for you. I heard it like thunder. He spoke Song of Solomon 8:6 and 7. Do you know those verses?"

Muttering some kind of affirmative response, Mike, still kneeling in prayer, looked down at the wedding card in his hand, shocked. His cheeks were still wet with the tears over prayers from these very verses, Song of Solomon 8:6–7.

Bob continued, "The Lord spoke that He was going to release grace for the message of these verses across the entire Body of Christ, worldwide. And He said He wants the message of Song of Solomon 8:6–7 to be the main focus of your ministry all the days of your life."

For Mike, that July day in the late eighties marked the beginning of just what the Lord had spoken: a lifelong pursuit and focus on the truth revealed about the heart of King Jesus and His Bride, the Church, in Song of Solomon 8:6–7. Since that day, he has given himself to countless hours of study, meditation, prayer and teaching from the book of Song of Solomon, seeing that the promise of the seal set upon the hearts of the entire Body of Christ to speak of the first commandment being restored to first place be *kept* in first place as the Lord's return draws near.

For my own life, this was the message that laid hold of me in my twenties; it was the truths that tore my heart open and awakened deepest yearnings for the fullness of knowing Jesus' immeasurable love, and later fueling the longings that wouldn't let go of me when I felt my passion waning. I believe first love is the first commandment kept in first place in a present-tense way. The seal of fire represents the flame of God's own love abiding in and keeping our love for Him. It also speaks of our voluntary love as we set Him and keep Him as the singular Reward of our lives, the Treasure of our souls.

> **I believe first love is the first commandment kept in first place in a present-tense way.**

The ancient seal was a wax seal used to encase royal documents such as a title deed or a military strategy. They were protected and authenticated by a royal seal. The king encased the royal document in wax. The king used his signet ring to seal the document, and that seal spoke of his guarantee that it was backed up by all the power of his kingdom. The seal spoken of in Song of Solomon 8:6 is not a seal of wax, but of divine fire. It is the love of God released by the power of Jesus through the Holy Spirit, inspiring fiery love in the heart of the Bride.

Jesus overcame the curse of death and the grave at the cross and resurrection with a love as strong as death and as jealous as the grave—that He might bring us into this overcoming, everlasting, burning love of the Godhead, the love shared between the Father and Son and Spirit of God. It takes God to love God, and out of His good pleasure and deep desire, the Father will put within us His own love for the Lord Jesus, causing our hearts to burn with the same passion and loyalty that He possesses for His Son. The very flame of God will be released in the human heart by the Holy Spirit, tenderizing our cold, dull hearts with God's own fiery affection.

He is committed to releasing this seal of love to our hearts. We, the redeemed, are invited to fellowship together with Him and one another in this Trinitarian love, producing abounding, internal joy in the hearts and lives of the Body of Christ. This fellowship and joy will become the inextinguishable power source that will empower His people to overcome the troubles that surge as many waters and floods at the end of the age, with an unoffended, unquenchable love (Revelation 12:11).

Our Radiant Future as Jesus' Inheritance

Our destiny as the Body of Christ is to live with hearts burning and caught up in the very love of the Godhead, both as individuals and together as one Body (John 15:9; 1 John 1:3). The highest priority of the Holy Spirit—to establish the first commandment in first place in the hearts of His people—does not begin with us, but with Him, as the God who abounded with perfect and wholehearted love within the fellowship of the Three Persons of the Trinity from everlasting (1 John 4:16). The command to love Him with all our heart, soul, mind and strength finds its source for fulfillment in the love that existed before the foundations of the world between the Father, the Son and the Holy Spirit. He desires and jealously requires our response of wholehearted love because

He Himself *is* wholehearted love—within the Godhead—and we were created in His image for such fervent love.

When Jesus prayed that the very love with which the Father loved Him would be in us, He spoke of the perfect love the Father had for Him from before the world was created. Jesus declared that He loves the redeemed in the same way and with the same intensity that His Father loves Him, and that the Father Himself loves the redeemed with the same love He has for His Son (John 15:9; 17:23).

From ages past, God the Father has promised His Son an inheritance. The angels did not even know it, but in the eternal counsels, God the Father decreed that an inheritance would be given to His Son and that this inheritance was already determined before the world was created. This inheritance was an eternal companion. It was a people who would be washed and cleansed and empowered by God to be joined to Jesus Christ as an equally yoked bride. He would have a suitable companion who would love Him with the same intensity that He loved her. She would love His Father in the way He loves His Father. She would enter her destiny of partaking of and expressing God's very own love, imparted to her by the Holy Spirit (Romans 5:5).

We were created in God's likeness, with the capacity to participate in this glorious love and fellowship, experiencing this most supreme joy and delight for which He fashioned us, and empowered to reciprocate and extend that love—both to God and to others—in response. This Trinitarian love is the fountain from which the Second Commandment—that we would love one another as we love ourselves—is fulfilled. Our love for others overflows from our experience of God's love (1 John 4:19). Abiding and partaking and imbibing deeply of this Trinitarian love is our only way forward into the victorious love for God and for one another that is our glorious calling and prophetic destiny together.

The Lord is leading the Body of Christ into a transformation of glorious oneness of heart and mind, just as He prayed for in John 17:23, and the source of that unity is the Trinitarian love and fellowship—filled with the very love of the Father for the Son, the love of the Son for the Father and the very love of God poured into our hearts by the Spirit.

It is when the Church comes into this destiny, and when she begins to walk in what Jesus' high-priestly prayer cried out for—that we would be one as the Father and Son are one and that the very love of the Father for the Son would be in us—that the world will behold and witness the greatest social miracle of all time. We will be one as the Father and Son are one, loving one another and even extending that same love to our enemies. This love that is set like a seal upon their heart and their arm—the inward affections and the outward actions—will put on display the wholehearted, sacrificial love of God Himself. Our light will so shine before men that they will see our good deeds and give glory to our Father in heaven (Matthew 5:15–16). We will shine as He shines in an environment growing dark. We will burn as He burns in a world growing cold.

A Light of Love Shining in Darkness

The night before Jesus was crucified, as they sat around the table, and just after Jesus had disclosed that one of His disciples would betray Him, Jesus spoke of the new commandment to love one another.

> Little children, yet a little while I am with you. You will seek me, and just as I said to the Jews, so now I also say to you, "Where I am going you cannot come." A new commandment I give to you, that you love one another: just as I have loved you, you also are to love one another. By this all people will know that you are my disciples, if you have love for one another.
>
> John 13:33–35 ESV

Later, the apostle John would call this new commandment *old* in that it was given from the beginning. At the same time, it was altogether *new* in Jesus and in those who are in Him. The light had now shone forth and pierced through the darkness.

Such self-giving love cannot be imitated but only *participated* in. It is *of God* and is the fruit of abiding in the True Vine, in Christ, and in His love (John 15:1–8; 1 John 4:7). Our love for one another, forgiving and covering sin and bearing long in love, is not an imitation of Jesus' love but a *manifestation* of it. This supernatural love is something utterly of God, *born* of God, and the *fruit* of abiding in deep relationship with Him. To love this way is miraculous and utterly impossible apart from Him (John 15:1–17). It is so stark and other-than and foreign to the fallenness and sin of man that Jesus said the world would know and recognize us to be His disciples by this radiant love we have for one another (John 13:35). The apostle John said that this new command is *true in Him and in us* because the darkness is already passing away, and the true light is already shining (1 John 2:8). When we love one another in obedience to this new commandment, His love is being perfected in us, and we are loving with His very love, bearing fruit to God and shining as lights in the world (John 15:16; 1 John 2:9).

What does this look like in our lives? First, we drink deeply of His deep love for us by meditating upon it, pondering it, dialoguing with the Lord in prayer over it and receiving it into our hearts each day. This love of the One who loved us and gave Himself for the Church, the Bride, is what cuts our hearts and rends them open with revelation. The light of His unmerited, forgiving love for us fills, overwhelms and tenderizes our hearts, and then we extend it toward one another. As we abide in it, the love of Christ for us pierces and changes us, bringing forth from our lives the same love for our brothers and sisters. And the light shines in the darkness. Death is overcome by life.

When we face conflicts with one another, we draw upon this undeserved love that we have received from God, and it enables us to prayerfully release to God those who have wronged us. It frees us to lay the offense at His feet, blessing the offenders in our hearts. It empowers us to go to the one who has offended us when needed, seeking to pursue love and peace in every relationship. Love becomes perfected in us as the fruit of forgiving love comes forth from our lives, glorifying the Lord and *proving* us to be His disciples.

Jesus spoke to His disciples of this love right before He would suffer and die and before they faced the trouble of being tested and scattered. These are the truths and the revelation we need to face our greatest troubles. As Jesus' return draws near, and testing and troubles increase, this is our way forward in love. In a world and culture where love is growing cold, God is zealous to raise up His Church—knit together in Christ—in the luminous light of divine love that triumphs, covering a multitude of sins.

Our *first love* for Him is both individual and bound together. We individually respond with all our hearts, and we watchfully guard, impart courage and strengthen one another in this holiest pursuit. The Lord will jealously bring forth His people as those whose love abounds more and more, growing increasingly fervent, even in the midst of trouble. He will produce in His Church those who have so been laid hold of by Christ's forgiving love that they extend it toward one another, and even to their enemies. This is the light of love we abide in and extend to our brother, overcoming every cause for stumbling. This is the love that never fails.

As darkness increases, the light of the love of Christ amidst His Church will also increase—a city on a hill that cannot be hidden. Defying the usual paths of increased coldness and dullness and deadness of heart, His Church will shine with a love that only abounds under pressure and amid the storms, a love that does not become "less and less" under pressure but "more and more," a love that does not draw back and decrease in the midst of trouble, but rather presses forward and increases. It expands in capacity and grows in fervency and sincerity, becoming a love that floods cannot drown and that many waters cannot quench (Song of Solomon 8:7).

A Fellowship That Breaks Forth in Joy

As we receive and express the love of God, in our own hearts and to others, we taste of the highest joys available to the human spirit and the most profound communion to be known among men—the fellowship of the saints of God by His Spirit. Freedom from offense and covering of sin are *only the beginning* of the glory we are invited into together as the Body of Christ. Unabashedly, the New Testament describes the light and love and joy that break forth as we abide in and experience the love of God and then overflow in love for one another in Christ. With a love centered in the burning fellowship of God's own love—the love between the Three Persons of the Godhead—one of the most precious realities in all existence is the shared communion of the saints in fellowship together with Christ. Participating in that fellowship together is what leads to *fullness of joy.*

John the apostle proclaimed, "What we have seen and heard we proclaim to you also, so that you too may have fellowship with us; and indeed, our fellowship is with the Father, and with His Son Jesus Christ. These things we write, so that our joy may be made complete" (1 John 1:3–4 NASB1995).

We are in Him, and He is in us, and because of that union and communion, we have fellowship with one another. Our closeness together comes out of our mutual bond in Christ, sharing of one Spirit, uniting us in a tremendous and deep relationship of love (1 Corinthians 12:13; Ephesians 4:4). It is a communion with origins not in one another, but in our mutual intimacy in Christ—making our friendship with one another profound and everlasting in nature (1 John 1:3). This deep bond creates joyful, affectionate and deep relationships with one another.

Girded with the forgiving love of Christ, we are equipped to continue in that bond of fellowship together, releasing one another from any resentments along the way. As we keep His commands to love Him and love one another, we find *fullness of joy*. Joy is one of the chief aims of the Holy Spirit and the great gifts of God to both strengthen and enable the hearts of His people to be liberated from the snares of offense, bitterness and fear. We walk in the light of fellowship, the passing from death to life, the perfecting of His love within us—that which arms us to have no fear in the day of judgment, filled with all confidence at His coming (John 15:11; 1 John 1:4, 7; 2:10, 28; 3:14–20).

> **Our closeness together comes out of our mutual bond in Christ, sharing of one Spirit, uniting us in a tremendous and deep relationship of love.**

Though the challenges of relationships have the power to ultimately shut down our hearts even to the Lord, they also have the potential to bring us nearer to the heart of Jesus than we've ever been. In those moments of heartache—when we truly love God and our greatest fear of all is losing touch with that tenderness in our hearts toward *Him*—is when the beauty of God is about to break forth from broken lives if we say *yes*. When our love runs dry of all its original steam is when we witness firsthand the Love that never fails, never wearies and never grows faint (1 Corinthians 13:8). When the cycle of self-reliance is broken and when we relinquish the constant fight to self-preserve, we can witness and stand in awe together of the mystery of the love of Christ—in all its heights and depths and lengths and widths—lavished on the undeserving and the broken. It's the love that surpasses knowledge yet is known by His saints (Ephesians 3:17–19).

As Jesus leaned in near to His disciples in those last moments with them before the command to love one another, He tied the walking out of those commands to fullness of joy. He said, "These things I have spoken to you, that my joy may be in you, and that your joy may be full" (John 15:11 ESV). Full joy is found in full love unto God and to one another. Jesus commands that which leads and keeps us on the path to full joy. Thus, our fight of faith and love—to remain in tenderness of heart, in fully alive and unhindered love, we will guard one another in Christ, seeking to persevere against unbelief and the snare of cynicism and bitterness, and loving one another with unguarded fervency—is not about just surviving but *thriving*. It is all about the abounding love and fruit of the Spirit filling us with love, joy, peace, patience, kindness and long-suffering. The One who created us knows what sin does to us, what unbelief and hardening do to the heart. His commands are unto the glorifying of His name and unto our *full joy* as we live as He created us to live and function.

Walking in this light of forgiving love through all the obstacles that we face and sharing in this joy of fellowship together in Christ, we are armed and equipped to fight and contend for one another in the Body of Christ with great passion and zeal. As members of one another, and with the Spirit binding our hearts together in the very love of God, we view each other through the tender lens of Jesus' own perspective. We see the beauty of Christ in one another and the gift each one brings, according to the grace of the Lord imparted to them (Ephesians 4:7). Having a revelation of our unity and dependency upon one another to be fully equipped and edified that we might come into the destiny that God desires for us, we come to recognize our profound need for—and our deficiency without—each one in the Body (Ephesians 4:12–15). This binding together in unity and oneness of heart and mind comes down to very practical love in our relationships with one another. And it is as we grow in becoming "keepers" of one another in the Body that we continue to shine forth the light of God and to experience the depths of joy that we were fashioned for (Genesis 4:9; 1 John 1:4).

Keeping One Another in the Fight of Faith

Sitting around my living room weekly, now for well over a decade, I have joined with godly comrades and friends who have held an irreplaceable voice into my heart and life at many key times. In the times when passion is under fire, and threatening winds of doubt or fear roll in uninvited, with the heart of Jesus, they have expressed words of life, prayed prayers of strengthening, and prophesied truths that imparted light and renewed confidence. Like witnesses that stand around and remind with the light of truth when we can't seem to find our way, our friends in Jesus are sovereignly given and greatly needed. Like ones who know the One we know and speak His heart—even when our own hearts can't recall His beautiful nature, His tender voice, His long-suffering affection, His gentleness and mercy—they speak. And when cynicism knocks, or offense threatens to bear the sour fruit of bitterness, these brothers and sisters in Christ come around us, as friends who refuse such adversaries to prevail over us. Few things are sweeter and more precious, few things bring greater joy to the heart, than this sharing in the fellowship of Christ, this keeping of one another in the fervent love of Christ.

Fellowship together with our brothers and sisters in the Body of Christ—speaking life and giving courage to each other—is one of the ways we ward off accusations and hardening of our hearts. Hearts stay tender and continue to drink of shared remembrance of Jesus' goodness when we walk closely together with others in Christ. This is why, apart from the attempt to sideline us in unbelief and offense as individuals, one of the chief aims of the enemy's tactics waged against us is to isolate us from or turn us against one another. This evil ambush is waged against our unity because it is in our oneness that we are able to stand strong, persevere and thrive in inward joy, regardless of circumstance. We greatly need each other in this pursuit of knowing and loving the Lord Jesus, in this race of enduring faith.

As we have seen, one of the greatest threats to our love for Jesus is that of unbelief. The thing that undermines our first love and causes us to draw back from Him is also what causes us to draw back from others. The Lord might say to us in these times of exposing the elusive, creeping unbelief within us: *You don't have a love problem but a faith problem.* That is what He said to me when He tenderly exposed the unbelief that had worked into the root system of my heart. When we lose our confidence, we begin to draw back, and that shrinking back of our hearts takes a heavy toll on our passion, our fresh love, and our tenderness of heart. This threat is something we guard against *together*, not just individually. It is a battle we fight collectively, not just alone.

In describing this danger of unbelief, the writer of Hebrews described how we are to watch over one another in this, guarding against the hardening of sin's deception, by exhorting one another daily. He warned:

> Beware, brethren, lest there be in any of you an evil heart of unbelief in departing from the living God; but exhort one another daily, while it is called "Today," lest any of you be hardened through the deceitfulness of sin. For we have become partakers of Christ if we hold the beginning of our confidence steadfast to the end.
>
> Hebrews 3:12–14

We are to *keep* one another in fervency and faith, and we need each other to ward off these subtle deceptions and snares. As His Bride and His Body, sharing in a God-given interconnectedness with our brothers and sisters in Christ, we are to strengthen one another in this way. When unbelief creeps in with its accusations of *He is not good* or *He is not true to His promise*, we need one another to ward off its threats. When unbelief lurks with cynicism and the accusations against God and one another, we need our brothers and sisters in Christ to see the threat and speak the truth in love to us.

The author of Hebrews goes on to describe how we have become partakers of Christ if we hold the beginning of our confidence steadfast to the end. Connecting this back to his prior instruction to exhort one another daily, we see Paul's insistence that keeping our fervent faith in Jesus is dependent on our brothers and sisters in Christ around us, purposefully strengthening and guarding one another in faith and love from encroaching, hardening unbelief.

Our faith in Jesus is not only benefited and strengthened by one another, but *reliant* upon and *bound* together. Without such togetherness, we will gradually drift from passion, from fervency, from vibrant confidence in Christ. We need to help guard and keep one another from the hardening that can set in without our realizing it. It is unbelief that makes us waver against the promise of God, and we need one another to wage warfare against that unbelief (Romans 4:20). Our fight is one of faith, and for that battle, we need our beloved brothers and sisters in Christ and are quite literally dependent upon them. From Jesus' perspective, as He looks upon us, He sees our lives not only individually, but as one. Our lives together are interwoven in Him, bound as one. We need each other for perseverance, for strengthening, and for the keeping of fervent love. We are to stir one another up toward love and good works (Hebrews 10:24). Our fellowship together is by no means optional or insignificant, but rather one of the crucial means that the Lord will employ to complete the good work He began in us at the day of Christ (Philippians 1:6).

Zealously Committed to One Another's Fullness

As members together in the Body of Christ, we are, in fact, one another's keeper (Genesis 4:9). The Lord wants to stir us with fervent devotion for each other in brotherly love—not stopping at keeping our words from accusing and doing harm but moving even further—into the glory of our calling to speak the truth over one another in love, to build one another up, according to each one's particular grace, given of God, that we might grow up in all things, with each part doing its share (Romans 12:10; Ephesians 4:7, 15–16, 29). We are to impart the same glorious love of Jesus to one another, seeing how He sees, speaking what He speaks, and loving how He loves. Jesus is the Head, the holy Husband, who washes His Bride by cherishing and nourishing her with the water of the Word. As members of one another, submitting to one another in the fear of the Lord, we are to love each other with this same love. We are to care and be committed to one another's fullness—all that Jesus fashioned each one for—and then fight for one another unto that end, until we all reach full maturity in love together.

The strategy of Satan, the accuser of the brethren, is that our mouths would be filled with accusation toward one another, and that divisions and strife would only increase in an hour when love is growing cold. Yet this is not our inheritance as those in Christ and as the dearly beloved ones to Jesus' heart. Our destiny is to have mouths filled with the very tender perspectives of Jesus over one another—speaking the prophetic heart of Christ in words of encouragement and divine insight over each other. To see each other as He sees us and to feel the very emotions that He feels for each one is our glorious inheritance as those in Christ, partaking of the same Spirit and drinking deeply of the same love.

One aspect of being members of one another is the way our very words are meant to build one another up in love and to keep one another from coming under the accusations of the enemy (Romans 14:19; 1 Thessalonians 5.11). My deliverance from the lies of accusation and the narrative of the enemy over my life is in the mouths of my brothers and sisters in Christ—as they speak, prophesy, encourage and intercede according to that narrative. In the same way, the narrative and declarations that Jesus speaks over each one, the fullness of their calling and full measure of the grace He has desired for them to walk in, are bound to those in the Body of Christ coming around them, viewing them as Jesus views them, speaking with the prophetic spirit the words that Jesus speaks over them and interceding according to the same burden and desires that the Great Intercessor prays for them. The fullness of our callings and destinies are bound together.

But how do we do this? How do we come out of our own opinions of one another and enter the perspectives and narrative of Jesus? First, we seek the Lord in prayer about one another in the Body of Christ, those friends and family that He has given us to walk with, and we ask Him to speak to us about these brothers and sisters in Christ. We ask: *Jesus, who is this person to You? What have You put within him or her that displays Your beauty? With what have You marked him? What grace have You given them? Show me the essence of who they are to You.* And the Lord answers by unveiling the beauty of one another to our eyes. In this way, we grow in knowing each other according to who we really are in the Spirit rather than according to the flesh (2 Corinthians 5:16).

Second, we ask one another: *What do you burn with? What has He marked you with? I am committed to your calling, to your destiny. I am committed to your coming into the fullness for which He laid hold of you* (Philippians 3:12). We press past the general understandings of one another, to lay hold of the specific graces and glories He has imparted to each one. Without that person coming into the full cultivation and maturity of that specific grace, without their imparting what Jesus has given them to the rest of the Body, we cannot become fully edified and grow up into the Head as one (Ephesians 4:15). We will be stunted. We need each one to come into the full measure of the grace Jesus has given them that we all might come into the fullness God has for us (Ephesians 4:13).

When I begin to see what Jesus has put in you, it quells any envy in me, because what He has put in you is unique and different and needed. I begin to recognize that there is a unique grace in you that I *need*. Eyes to see the beauty in one another thwarts the comparison, the rivalry, the envy—all the things that keep us in the opposite spirit of love and unity. Instead, we become filled with fervent, tender, sacrificial affection for one another, willing to fight for each other—not for ourselves or our own calling—but to see another's greatness.

We will get and stay free from competition and strife by the revelation of the unity of our value and purpose before God. We will also be empowered to rejoice in the prosperity of other believers, churches, and ministries as we grow in the revelation of the body of Christ. We will see their prosperity as our prosperity because we see the body as one practical unit seeking the same end in every geographic area. A believer with this revelation will automatically feel grieved at everything that divides or injures the unity of the body by undermining one of its members. They see division as injuring the physical expression of Jesus' life on earth. The church is made up of weak and imperfect humans, but it is so much more than merely a human institution. It is the holy expression on earth of His heavenly life. We are more than just individual believers. We are members of one another; therefore, we literally belong to one another. This gives us a mutual identity and responsibility for each other (Genesis 4:9).[1]

We call one another forth and we keep guard over one another from the evil one. We ask our brother or sister what the accusation is that the enemy often whispers in their ear. When we know these lies, we are armed to combat them with truth. This takes vulnerability and a great measure of openheartedness toward each other, yet such transparency is the way we contend against the schemes of the enemy to silence and prevail over individuals. Though this puts me in a vulnerable position to tell you the precious things Jesus has marked me with or to share where the arrows of darkness often lodge in me, sharing these insights with my brothers and sisters in Christ frees them to stand guard with me—both over the gift of God in me and against the assault of the enemy.

When we come into this revelation of how we are to be one another's keeper, we come into the understanding of how we *all* suffer if even one of us gets shut down by the evil one. If Jesus' specific grace in that person's life is sabotaged by the enemy and his evil statements about their future, we cannot grow up together into mature love and fullness. We are deficient as the Body of Christ unless each one does his part, and thus we contend for one another in intercession, warring against the accusations of the enemy. Speaking the truth in love over one another, that we might each offer that particular part He has graced us with, we grow up in maturity into the Head together (Ephesians 4:15).

Comprehending His Love Together

Not only is our fellowship together in Christ a means of upholding our perseverance and safeguarding our faith in Christ, but it is *together*, and not separate from one another, that we touch and experience the bursting comprehension of the love of Christ, unto the very fullness of God (John 15:11; Ephesians 3:16–19).

For the church of Ephesus, Paul prayed:

For this reason I bow my knees to the Father of our Lord Jesus Christ, from whom the whole family in heaven and earth is named, that He would grant you, according to the riches of His glory, to be strengthened with might through His Spirit in the inner man, that Christ may dwell in your hearts through faith; that you, being rooted and grounded in love, may be able to comprehend with all the saints what is the width and length and depth and height—to know the love of Christ which passes knowledge; that you may be filled with all the fullness of God.

Ephesians 3:14–19

There are many things to draw from this glorious prayer—a portion of Scripture that elevates our vision to the highest heights of the Christian life, the mountaintop of Christian experience. Yet within this summit prayer, we find the truth that the heights of our experiential joy in knowing the love of Christ are found not in isolation but *together* with all the saints. After praying that Christ would take up abode and dwell within their hearts—by His Spirit, settling down and being at home there—Paul prayed for the comprehension of this love *together with all the saints*. Though this means that all the saints of Christ are to know and experience this profound love, it also points to the truth of how we are bound to one another in this glorious comprehension. It is *together* that we enter in to knowing this full measure of the love of Christ.

We are so profoundly bound together in Christ that we are called His Body—a picture of the Bride of Christ dwelling in unity together. Together, we are His Body and "members individually" (1 Corinthians 12:27). Through His death on the cross, believers in Him share in a mystery of unity by His Spirit. Together, we are members of His Body, of His flesh, and of His bones (Ephesians 5:30–32). "We are members of one another"

(Ephesians 4:25). His body was torn on the cross that we might together be brought into the unity and oneness that only comes from God. He is the One who loved us and washed us from our sins in His own blood, that we might extend that very love to one another.

We together are the Church, the Bride, for whom the Bridegroom gave His life in death. As the greater Hosea, He paid the price for our ransom with His very own life—to redeem a harlot bride, Jew and Gentile, for Himself. We share in that history and that identity, together. Not one of us deserving. Not one of us radiant in the beginning of the story. All of us sinners. All of us having fallen short of the glory of God. We all stand together before the Bridegroom's cross, the holy Husband, the Head of the Church, and we marvel with hearts torn open at His passionate, tender love for us. All of us need His love to cover over the multitude of our sins, of His washing us with water by His Word, of His cherishing and nourishing us as we grow into mature love. We together are His Bride, chosen in Him before the foundation of the world that we might be presented to Him pure, spotless and radiant.

Perhaps this is one reason why Paul spoke of the experiential knowledge of Christ's love being something we enter *together* and not just as individuals. Though we know His love independently from one another, by His Spirit poured out in our hearts, we also know it by the shared fellowship in His Spirit that we partake of together. We are being fitted and built *together* as "a dwelling place of God in the Spirit" (Ephesians 2:20–22). We are mysteriously one with Him and together His mystical Body. As Paul said, *"This is a great mystery, but I speak concerning Christ and the church"* (Ephesians 5:32). Our love for Him is inseparably bound to our love for one another, and we cannot love God without loving our brother. We cannot love our brother unless we abide in the love of God. And, *together*, we comprehend and know the love of Christ.

Often, we don't run the race of loving one another with the necessary endurance because we have either lost or never seen the finish line of that race. We have forgotten or do not yet have a biblical perspective of where this love is headed. What is the finish line? The narrative of Scripture assures us of a breathtaking, soul-converting, radiant, and splendid love that will arise from the Body of Christ like a beacon in the storm before the Lord's return at the end of the age.

We will be a burning and shining people made up of every ethnicity, every language, every denomination, bought by the blood of Christ and bound together in Him. Descriptions like "radiant," "without spot," and "glorious"—and with a witness that soundly converts the unbelieving world—are not overstatements or just grandiose language. In fact, language is, and will be, insufficient to describe what Jesus' Church will become in its full maturity. Of the love that she will know and experience and abound in, Paul said it is exceedingly above all that we can ask or think, according to the power that works in us. It passes knowledge, but by His Spirit in the inner man, He will strengthen us with might to comprehend it. We will burn within with a love that many waters cannot quench, keeping Him as our highest Treasure, the great Reward of our lives. We will comprehend together—with all the saints—the vast width, the exceeding length, the profound depth, and the endless height of the love of Christ.

This love, known and comprehended together in Christ, arising from a peculiar people and nation made up of every denomination and culture, every nation and tongue, will be something the world has never seen. Though there have been radiant lights all throughout church history, as the end of the age draws near, a culminating and piercing light of love, from the people of God, will shine forth in brightest witness amidst the darkest hour of history. And the world will know and believe that God has sent His Son, because of the love they have for one another—the love that is God's own love within them and among them, set like a seal upon their hearts, a most vehement flame that many waters cannot quench (Song of Solomon 8:6, 7).

PRAYER

Jesus, let Your love be like a fiery seal upon my heart, that I would love You with the very love of the Godhead—that it would burn in me. Catch me up in the sweetness and consolation of the fellowship of Your love, the very flame of God that burns like an interior fire in me, the love that even the many waters of trouble or persecution or offense cannot quench. Let me carry this fervent love for my sisters and brothers in the Body of Christ, interceding for and speaking the truth of Your heart over them, until we all come to the complete unity that You have for us.

STEPS FORWARD IN KEEPING PASSION FOR JESUS

- Ask the Lord to set His love as a seal upon your heart—the love that many waters cannot quench, that the first commandment would be in first place in your heart and life. Invite Him to cause your heart to burn with the very love the Father possesses for His Son (Song of Solomon 8:6, John 17:26). Consider making this prayer one that you return to over and over, throughout all your days.
- Ask the Holy Spirit to open your eyes to see the beauty He sees in two or three specific brothers and sisters in Christ. As He shows you His heart for them, pray about speaking some of these things to them, with a heart to build them up in the Lord.

10

Burning with Unquenchable Love until He Comes

The pages of this book were not written from a safe distance, but in the rawness of real time, chapter by chapter, as I lived their unfolding page by page. Sometimes books are written not with preplanned outlines, but with headlong launching into their unknown course. When I first began to put words together concerning Jesus' call to keep *first love* from Revelation 2, I was more heartbroken about having seemingly lost it than I was faith-filled that He would give me grace to return to it and keep it. I didn't know the path forward. Yet the pen forged ahead, because I knew in my heart that His Word does not lie, and for what He commands, He gives abundant grace to which to respond. I believed He was more jealous than I was to keep my heart alive. And with that mustard seed–sized faith in my hand, I pressed into His grace.

Still, I began the path almost *hurt* by the Lord for asking something so impossible of me—of us all. Something had gone wrong with my passion and childlike trust even though I had fought with all my heart to keep it alive. Though I had a history of loving these words Jesus spoke to the church of Ephesus, because of the way they so communicate His desire for His people, I felt injured by them. Then, feeling so personal and cutting, they seemed to me to be almost harsh in their unattainability.

Had I known then what I know now, I would have told my past self, *Hang on! It's going to be okay! He is going to restore your heart! What you don't know yet, but He will show you over time, is that you unwittingly let some unbelief creep in, and it dampened your affections. Without recognizing it, you gave space to the voices of accusation—both inward and outward. And over time you concluded that Jesus felt the same of you as those disapproving voices. Gradually, you quit believing and receiving at the gut level His delight over you, shutting down your heart in the distance. But it's all right! Because He is so kind—kinder than you'd even believed. There's going to be a journey, and it's going to be His lovingkindness that will light the path. He will shine forth the gentleness that never wavered since the moment He first tenderized your heart, all those years ago. Graciously, He will shine His light upon your wrong ideas of Him, where you made agreements with unbelief. And His kindness will lead you to repentance. His tenderness with you will surprise and heal your heart. Sit before Him. Wait upon Him. Feed upon His Word and cry out to Him. He'll do the things He did at first so that you can do the things you did at first. He will draw you back by reopening those early hungers and desires for Him and by showing you how He has not changed His mind. He will renew your faith as you repent of unbelief and return to childlike trust. He will ignite passion by reminding you of His unreserved and ardent affection and the delight that has never wavered. He renews the strength of those who wait on Him. He lifts them up with wings like eagles. He restores their souls! Hang on! Love is not lost. In fact, it is only at its beginning.*

Tears of gratitude stream as I write this because that is what He has done in me. He took a wilted soul and restored it to its deep, interior joy. Taking His Word and wrestling over His command-turned-into-promise, I sat before Him in prayer, Bible and heart wide open, over weeks and months. And He took my injured, debilitated heart and healed it. He took the flickering flame that was my love and fanned it into full fire again. He restored the passion. The delight. The confidence. The faith. The childlike trust. The openheartedness. Now I can kneel on the ground beside Isaiah, and with experiential knowledge as never before, I am able to say along with him:

> The LORD is the everlasting God, the Creator of the ends of the earth. He does not faint or grow weary; his understanding is unsearchable. He gives power to the faint, and to him who has no might he increases strength. Even youths shall faint and be weary, and young men shall fall exhausted; but they who wait for the LORD shall renew their strength; they shall mount up with wings like eagles; they shall run and not be weary; they shall walk and not faint.
>
> Isaiah 40:28–31 ESV

I stand in the throng beside David and join him in proclaiming:

> Bless the LORD, O my soul; and all that is within me . . . who redeems your life from destruction, who crowns you with lovingkindness and tender mercies, who satisfies your mouth with good things, so that your youth is renewed like the eagles.
>
> Psalm 103:1–5

A Bright and Shining Church

When I felt pain over the seeming diminishing of my love for Jesus, I not only was strengthened by Jesus' command to return to first love—seeing in His call a promise of His grace to *keep* it—but I found assurance by what the Word of God reveals of the Church and where He is leading her as His return draws near. To possess and keep first love in devotion to Jesus is not simply the ideal for the individual heart; it's the undeniable future of the Church. My heart's renewal and your heart's reviving to the place of fervent passion, loyalty and childlike faith are only part of the bigger story. Personal revival into fervent love is the starting point for our glorious future together: the Church made ready for the Lamb of God.

His Word is true, and if what the New Testament pronounces of the victorious Church before the Lord's return is so certain, we can be confident of His jealousy to bring forth every heart and life of His people unto that glorious end. The enemy would seek to convince us that we are disqualified from these future promises, but such accusations lose their power when held up against the brilliant and undeniable destiny of God's people pronounced in His Word. Perhaps the greatest argument for why we never have to lose our first love is that *this radiant future* the Bible proclaims is sure and certain.

The Church at the end of the age will be characterized by fierce loyalty and devotion to Jesus, living wholly unto the Lord, with the first commandment in first place and *first love* on full display. Over and over, the New Testament proclaims these truths. It brings us to the balcony view of beholding our marvelous destiny, the day when Christ will present to Himself a radiant Church, not having spot or wrinkle or any such thing, but holy and without blemish, blameless and above reproach in His sight (Ephesians 5:27; Colossians 1:22).

The breathtaking descriptions of God's people in mature love before His return are so extravagant that we often don't know what to do with them. We look at the state of the Church and at our own lives and can't fully grasp how He could possibly take His Church from where we are, in dullness, division and distraction, to what His Word promises we will be: alive in loyal love, united as one, watchful in prayer and perseverant through troubles. To believe these are real and true promises—that He will bring to pass—causes us to live wounded with a vision so magnificent, pained over the gaps we see in our current state, yet also filled with expectant faith, hope and joy as to what He will do—and what He won't hold back—to bring us forth in full splendor.

The Delight and Gentleness That Matures and Beautifies Us

The question that arises as we consider this glorious future of a Church in mature love is: *How will He do it?* How will He bring you and me, weak and ordinary as we are, and the Church at large, broken and flawed as she is, from where we are presently to the destination the New Testament describes? How will He do what Paul described when he spoke of bringing the Church across the nations into the full measure of maturity in Christ (Ephesians 4:13)? I believe Ephesians 5:29 holds an essential answer to these questions.

In this most premier passage in the New Testament revealing Jesus as the Bridegroom and the Church as the Bride, Paul described the way Jesus would do the unthinkable: bring forth His Church in splendor. The Husband who loved the Church and gave Himself for her, the One who is leading her to the day when He will present her to Himself a glorious Church without spot or wrinkle, holy and without blemish, leads her to that day in a very *specific* way. Sanctifying and cleansing her with the washing of the water of His Word, He tenderly leads her *by nourishing and cherishing her*. He leads her by expressing Himself with His cherishing, tender words of affection (Ephesians 5:26).

Knowing and experiencing His delight in enjoyment of us, even in our weakness, while we are not yet mature but on our way to mature love, is the very thing that will mature our love for Him. As believers who sincerely love Him, those for whom He shed His holy blood to wash and redeem and sanctify, He doesn't just legally love or simply tolerate. He delights in us. *Today*. Though we are not yet fully mature, He sees in us that beautiful inheritance the Father promised Him and that He gave His life to ransom. He enjoys us as we are growing in Him. He delights in us even when we, as genuine lovers of God, come up short and feel accused.

We see our brokenness and our weakness, yet in these deficiencies, He wants us to receive His tender, transforming love. This holy and undeserved delight, in the midst of our immature but growing love, is the very catalyst that will bring us into *mature* love for Him, enabling us to overcome every obstacle and every sin that entangles. With a continual tasting of the undeserved mercy and gentleness we were given at the cross, we remember, receive and abide in the kindest and most merciful love ever to break forth into the dark night of human history. And it becomes the power source for growing up into the Head.

By revealing His affections as the Bridegroom for His Church, He washes and renews us and will make us mature in love.

By revealing His affections as the Bridegroom for His Church, He washes and renews us and will make us mature in love. When we face our immaturity, our failures, and our weakness, it is Jesus' delight and joy over us, as He receives our willing spirit to be His, that matures our love for Him. It is His deep knowing of who we are as His Bride that brings us forth in blamelessness and holiness before Him and in undying love for one another. By speaking and revealing His tender affections, His cherishing love and His enjoyment of us—offered to us even while we are yet immature and weak—He causes us to walk in *joy* and *confidence* and to impart that same cherishing love to others.

The revelation of who He is as the Bridegroom is the burning light and experiential consolation that will bring forth a perfected and mature love in the Church. She will know His affection over her as the One who calls her "Married," and "My delight is in her," and that affection will beautify her as she partners with His grace and grows in love and humility.

The One who leads us is the One wholly committed to bringing us forth into mature love. With delight, He passionately directs our lives to bring us into the radiant future of a pure and spotless bride in full splendor and in full agreement with Him. His leadership is like gold, refined and pure and without fault. Without violating our free will, and continually pulling upon the cords of voluntary love in our hearts, He draws us after Himself throughout our lives. He leads us by tenderly cherishing and delighting in us, washing us with the water of His Word, every step of the way. This holy, tender, cherishing love that He extends to us all along the way, in times of weakness, in times of feeling exposed for our spiritual lack, in times when we come up short, is the power source for our sustained first love. This is the love we abide and remain in, warding off the accusations, the shame, the condemnation and the unbelief that would seek to destroy it. This is the fountain from which we draw, as we have already considered, in the most difficult relational fractures and betrayals we face.

Critical to having our hearts thrive and flourish amid the pressures and disruptions and exposures—both that we are presently walking through and that which we will face increasingly in the days ahead—is deeply knowing the delight of Jesus, leading to confidence in His love. This isn't something we begin with and then leave behind. It isn't something from which we graduate or even from which we have the option to grow distant. His delight in us as the very ones He has redeemed, purchased and sanctified is a delight we are to drink from every step of the way, to abide in at all times. His enjoyment of us—His gracious evaluations of our sincere, but immature love—is the very thing that will bring us from *sincerity* to *maturity*. It is the very thing that will wash our view of one another, enabling us to see each other with tender enjoyment, even in our weaknesses and immaturity, until the day we come into the fullness of mature love, as His beautiful Bride (Revelation 19:7–9; 22:17).

A Bride Made Ready

The New Testament depicts this state of maturity of the Church at the end of the age as that of *a bride made ready.* The Body of Christ, no matter their ages or personal histories, will corporately carry the quintessential qualities of an engaged bride. She will be loyal and fervent in love. She will be made ready for Him with a love that is undivided, unrestrained and full. She loves what He loves and hates what He hates. This is the day of the gladness of His heart, the glorious day (Revelation 19:7).

As His Church, we will increasingly comprehend who He is as the Bridegroom and who we are as His Bride. This revelation and understanding of our identity before Him will function as an indispensable catalyst in bringing forth our faithful, mature love for Jesus, as we draw close to the hour of His appearing.

Before Jesus returns, this Bride in full maturity will come forth in the grace of God and by the power of His Spirit. Jesus died to bring her into this glorious maturity. We can be confident that the Lord will do what He has purposed and promised to do. He will carry out the very desires and zeal of His heart. And out of the wilderness of this age, a Bride made ready for the Lamb, leaning in dependency upon Him and radiant with mature love for Him, will arise—a fully prepared, glorious Church (Song of Solomon 8:5; Ephesians 5:27)!

Jesus' eyes look with piercing focus upon His glorious future day. When He will come. When His Church will be made ready. When He will ride upon the clouds in splendor, the saints who have died first with Him. When those in Christ who are alive on the earth will arise to meet Him in the air, their bodies changed in the twinkling of an eye. When He will march through the land in indignation and conquer every foe that stood in opposition to His love and His Kingdom. When at last, the ultimate fulfillment of the great wedding feast will come, and the Father will proclaim, "All things are ready. Come to the wedding!" (1 Corinthians 15:52; Habakkuk 3:12; Matthew 22:4).

The One who now sits at the right hand of the Father, the One who first awakened our hearts with fervent love, has not changed. And though we live now in the delay He often spoke of preceding His return, He wants our love not to grow old or cold in the waiting, but to be ever vibrant, burning brighter and brighter unto the perfect day. Just as we are not to interpret His delay as His indifference or passivity, we are not to imagine He has grown distant from His own passionate love for us that so stirred our hearts in the beginning.

God's Word makes it clear that *first love* is not only a reference back to our own individual stories and journeys in Jesus but speaks of the *quality* of love God is after in His Church at large. He is preparing us for Himself with a love that mirrors His passion, a desire that echoes and exonerates His desire. And therefore He puts within us His own inexorable, unrelenting, unwearied, holy love. He is getting us ready for Himself, just as He promised (Ephesians 5:27; Revelation 19:7–9).

A Unified, Holy Aching

One of the chief qualities of the love we will possess for Jesus as He brings us into maturity by His grace is that of *longing* for Him and for His return. Jesus will come to a Bride who is made ready and longing for Him to come again and unified in that longing. The end of the story reveals the Church together crying out with the Spirit of God, "Come, Lord Jesus." They have found Him to be their greatest treasure and delight and the One their soul loves (Psalm 37:4; Song of Solomon 3:2–3; Matthew 6:20–21).

Mature love is simultaneously *matured desire*. And Jesus leads us in such a way to bring longing into fullness. The first commandment expressed in maturity—to love the Lord with all our heart, soul, mind and strength—is also *desire* at full capacity. Full love must be undergirded by full desire. We want Jesus with all our beings, all of our affections. Our inward capacities are made wide and enlarged, and our panting souls are thirsty for God alone. This is what we see at the end of the story, when Jesus brings His Church into fully mature love, prepared and made ready to be presented to Him, glorious and without blemish (Ephesians 5:27).

In Revelation 22:17, at the close of the entire written Word of God, we see where we are headed, both individually and corporately—the finish line that Jesus in His perfect leadership is shepherding every believer toward. We see the Church made ready with full love and full desire, in unity with the Holy Spirit, crying, "Come!"

> And the Spirit and the bride say, "Come!" And let him who hears say, "Come!" And let him who thirsts come. Whoever desires, let him take the water of life freely.

Inherent in this future maranatha-cry that will proceed from the Spirit and Bride is a deep knowing of the Lord. It is a holy groaning that arises from having truly tasted of Him by the Spirit and having seen His beauty and worth with the eyes of faith. The New Testament apostolic prayers will come into their momentous fulfillment, with the spirit of wisdom and revelation in the knowledge of Jesus resting upon the Church. With the eyes of her heart enlightened, she will know the hope of His calling and the riches of His glorious inheritance in His saints. She will know the immeasurable greatness of the power of the One whom the Father gave to the Church, as Head over all things (Ephesians 1:17–19).

With all the saints together as one, the Church will come into that glorious inward strengthening to comprehend the breadth and length, the height and depth of the love of Christ (Ephesians 3:16–19). The Spirit of God delights to glorify Jesus in our hearts, magnifying Him and making Him known to us (John 14:26; 1 Corinthians 2:9–12). Out of the substance of true relational knowledge of Jesus will arise a lovesick, all-consuming, unified, desirous cry. This isn't an uninformed desire. This isn't a cry for only some aspects of Jesus. She knows whom she is asking the Father to send. Out of every tribe and nation will come forth this comprehensive calling out for Jesus to return, an eruption of holy longing and agreement that directly triumphs over Satan's ancient strategy since the Garden: to convince man to reject God.[1]

Jesus described the days between His two comings as the days when friends of the Bridegroom will mourn for Him, living lives of fasting and yearning as His friends, longing for the day of His appearing. This was the maranatha-heart that fueled the apostles of the early Church as they gave themselves to the preaching and spreading of the Gospel. Having known and loved the Son of God, they yearned for the day of His appearing and burned with passion that He receive the reward of His inheritance: a worthy Bride, made ready (Matthew 9:15; John 3:29; 2 Corinthians 11:2).

The Lord is bringing forth this same heart in His people, His friends, as His return draws near. As His friends, we will long for Him to come, and we will give ourselves in radical abandonment to preparing and making ready the Bride for

Him. We will live in deep yearning for His return. Jesus not only desired friends at His first coming; He wants friends now. He desires a lovesick bride—a yearning Church. And He will not return without it. He has set His heart upon it, prophesied it and jealously works within our hearts by His Spirit to bring it forth (Matthew 9:15; 22:37; Revelation 22:17).

The end of the story reveals a people who have put off and overcome the accusations of the evil one—those directed toward God, toward themselves and toward others—that enflamed and divided and defeated. Having become strong in the love arising from the crucified Bridegroom's shed blood, they have covered a multitude of sins in love for one another, bound together in holy, blood-bought unity. Together, out of this deep love, united hearts and wholehearted devotion for Jesus, they long for His return. As John Piper said:

> The Bridegroom left on a journey just before the wedding, and the Bride cannot act as if things are normal. If she loves Him, she will ache for His return. . . . Saving faith says, "Thy kingdom come! Come back, O precious Bridegroom. Come, reign as King. Come, vindicate your people. Come, marry your bride."[2]

In that day, each member of the Body and individual believer will have tended to the holy aching for the Son of God, carefully keeping the fire of first love for Jesus burning. By His grace, we will not lose our way but keep our first love all our days. Preserving tenderness and sensitivity to God continually, embracing love and humility and holding close to our hearts the dream to love Him entirely—in full givenness—we will move forward into this future together. We will love Him without division, without fractures and with all that we are from the depths of our beings—just as we were made to. Having called every other pleasure as worthless compared to the sweetness of His love, and having faced many pressures and persecutions and considered them joy for the sake of love, the loyalty and devotedness of our love for Him will be breathtaking in its splendor—a love made worthy of the Lamb (2 Thessalonians 1:11–12; James 1:2–4).

An abounding ache will consume the hearts and lives of the Bride of Christ throughout all the nations, and she will cry out from every part of the earth in invitation for God to return to the earth. From the midst of the darkest night in human history—days filled with persecution and martyrdom of God's people under the reign of the Antichrist—will come forth this piercing light of love, this unprecedented song of loyal affection and devotion to Jesus.

> Biblically, we are called to live like an engaged woman anticipating her wedding day, but too many believers live like a married woman remembering. We tend to think of the day we are saved as the great event in our lives, but that is simply not true. The day we are saved is the day God began His work to prepare us for the great day coming. A Christian who is not interested in the return of Jesus is like a bride not interested in her wedding day; it is abnormal. Sadly, many in the church do not think often about Jesus' return because the subject has been neglected or taught in an unbiblical way. However, when it is taught in a biblical way, it should create a deep longing in our hearts and provoke us to engage in God's mission to prepare the earth for the return of the Son.[3]

No longer will there be a Church in the earth that is generally content to live with things as they are. No longer will she live disconnected from the wedding day, indifferent to her glorious future, and dulled from the desire for Jesus to come. Rather, she will be as a bride no longer able to accept the separation from her Bridegroom, living with intense desire and eager anticipation for the day of His return.

Jesus' eyes will search the earth, and no longer will He find His people passionless and indifferent, with divided affections.

She will not be lured to sleep by the world or adulterated by other passions. Rather, she will love with pure and entire affection, just as He called her to. She will long for Him with full, undivided desire, beckoning Him to return. And He will answer that cry with His majestic appearing.

First Love at the End of the Story

It is not only individuals returning to a love that they first offered and received in the Lord, but an innumerable multitude of people, made up of every tongue and tribe, lifting their hearts of adoration and worship to God, with one voice and one heart and full givenness to Jesus.

Collectively, she is as a bride betrothed; and as one, she lifts her voice of full passion, full trust and full agreement. She is as one who has returned to the initial lovesickness, the initial desires, the initial burnings and affections that she was created to possess from the opening of time. Her light of love for Him and for others fills the earth and breaks forth in radiant proclamation of His work and splendor. She looks and sounds like Him, with a voice of many waters and garments made white by His blood and by her righteous deeds, done in love for Him (Revelation 19:7–9).

What we began with—that Jesus only commands what He gives us every grace to obey—we see in full splendor at the end of the story. He commanded that we love Him with everything. He commanded that we love one another as He loved us. Here we see the promised future of the Body of Christ, at the end of the age, in overcoming love, unoffended and shining in full glory.

Though having walked through the bleakest hour of all time, with more tribulation and persecution of the saints than any previous generation, the Church will shine forth in unity and in love that is not only without offense but in deep agreement and partnership with Him. Their love and loyalty for Jesus will not only survive the trouble but *thrive* during it. Far beyond toleration or hesitant submission, they will glory in His leadership with a heart of adoration. With a love worthy of the Lamb, they will be loyal to Him.

This love will not only be expressed with our hearts but demonstrated by our very lives. Having been forever pierced by the love of the Bridegroom, having been given entrance to the deep affections and desires of His heart, we will not only be made ready to love Him with fierce and fervent love but to give our very lives for Him and for one another. His love is as strong as death, equipping us for whatever we face in pressure, in persecution, in suffering, even if it means to stand among those described in Revelation 12:11, loving not our lives even unto death (Song of Solomon 8:6).

> The end-time Church will be marked by martyrdom because she will be mature in love for Jesus. Confronted with persecution, suffering, conflicts, and numerous testings, many will lose their lives for their faithfulness and devotion to Jesus. They will overcome the opposition of the antichrist by the blood of the Lamb and by the word of their testimony, loving not their lives unto death (Revelation 12:11). Such vibrancy and allegiance to Jesus are qualities not of a weak and passionless people, but of one that is thriving in love and faithfulness unto Jesus. In the midst of hostile circumstances and conflicts, the Lord will release great power and glory on His people. They will know their God, stand firm in persecution, and actively instruct many in the Word, and in righteousness (Daniel 11:32–33; 12:3).[4]

In an unparalleled time of trouble, the Church will come into her full glory and maturity, lifting her voice from the ends of the earth, in songs that proclaim the glory of the Lord (Isaiah 24:16; 60:2). The prophets called this unprecedented time a day of trouble and distress, a day of darkness and not light (Amos

5:18; Zephaniah 1:15–16). Jesus called it a tribulation such as has not occurred since the beginning of the world, until now, and never will again (Matthew 24: 21). It will be a time when Satan will operate with great wrath because he will realize his time is short. Yet even in this darkest hour, Scripture reveals that the people of God will be victorious in love for Him, with an unoffendable love, giving witness to His beauty and worth for all the world to hear and behold (Isaiah 24:14–16; Daniel 12:3; Revelation 12:11).

> **Yet even in this darkest hour, Scripture reveals that the people of God will be victorious in love for Him, with an unoffendable love, giving witness to His beauty and worth for all the world to hear and behold.**

From the ends of the earth, out of every tribe and tongue, will arise what the psalmist declared:

Worship the LORD in the splendor of holiness. . . . Say among the nations, "The LORD reigns! . . . He will judge the peoples with equity." Let the heavens be glad, and let the earth rejoice. . . . For he comes to judge the earth. He will judge the world in righteousness, and the peoples in his faithfulness.

Psalm 96:9–13 ESV

Again, it is not a weak, dull, divided Church that we find at the end of the story. Rather, it is one thriving in love—for God, for one another and for enemies. In an hour of love growing cold and a time of great darkness and escalation of evil, the Church will shine with purity and holiness and the very light of God. Standing firm in fervent devotion and joy, Jesus will be glorified in her as she unwaveringly and sacrificially responds righteously and humbly to suffering and unjust oppression.

And from the poured-out lives of God's people, the ends of the earth will behold the glorious witness of the matchless worth of Christ (Matthew 5:14).

He Will Return to a Bride in First Love

Today, we are to live in perpetual first love because, until the day He comes, we await the glorious wedding day with the same focus and tenacity that a young, betrothed woman awaits her wedding day. To grow weary in fervent desire would be like a bride showing up to the altar and confessing that she got tired of waiting. As a corporate, lovesick, intercessory cry arises from the end-time Church to Jesus, the One seated on the throne will behold His Bride, His inheritance in the saints who are from every tongue and tribe. The Bride will be loving and worshiping Him with all her heart, soul, mind and strength—just as His great command prophesied would come forth from His people. Her worship will ascend in one voice before Him, loyal and faithful and true, declaring her absolute agreement with Jesus and His ways, even His plan to come and remove from the earth all that hinders love, judging His enemies and riding forth victoriously as the mighty Warrior Judge (Psalm 45:3–5; Revelation 19:1–3).

One in their affection and in their blood-bought unity, their lives will embody a corporate glorifying of God and holy aching that says, *You, Jesus, are our first love. Your love is better than wine. Your lovingkindness is better than life. You are Chief among ten thousand. You are fairer than the sons of men. Your leadership is perfect, like gold refined. You are the One whom we love. You are the King whom we want. You are our soul's desire.*

The Lord Jesus, so indescribably moved over the love, worship and intercession of His beloved Bride, will declare over us, "You have ravished my heart, my sister, my spouse; you have ravished my heart with one look of your eyes. . . . Who is she who looks forth as the morning, fair as the moon, clear as the

215

sun, awesome as an army with banners?" (Song of Solomon 4:9; 6:10). I imagine a cry coming forth from His divine heart, so moved by the love of His people: "Father! She is ready! How she loves Me! How she has responded to My love and My grace. Isn't she lovely? Oh, the riches of the glory of My inheritance in these ones, the saints, My beloved. The very love that You have for Me is in them. Father, can I go to them?" And the Father, overjoyed in pleasure over the beauty of His sons and daughters, this inheritance that He was so jealous to bring forth for His worthy Son—now prepared and made ready as a suitable partner for Him—will say, "It is time."

> Isaiah 42 tells us that Jesus' return is a response to a cry of worship and intercession on the earth. The chapter begins with the prediction of the beauty of God's Servant (Jesus). In light of the beauty of God's Servant, Isaiah commanded the nations to sing from the very ends of the earth and associated this extravagant singing with the return of the Lord. In response, Jesus will release His own cry that is compared to the cry of a "woman in labor." The strength of Jesus' response tells us quite a bit about the strength of the church's cry. God will cry out in His strength because the church will have cried out in hers.[5]

Responding to the wholehearted cry of His people, the beloved Son of God, who for a long time has held His peace, will cry out like a woman in labor. Bursting with the jealous and tender passion that has filled the being of the Godhead from everlasting, He will answer the cry of His people—the songs arising from His Church throughout the nations and from the ends of the earth. In answer to His beloved ones, having hastened the day of the Lord with their holy love, Jesus will break forth like a mighty man, stirring up His zeal like a man of war, armed with strength to prevail over His enemies, to take His place as King over all the nations and to usher in the day of the gladness of His heart (Song of Solomon 3:11; Isaiah 42:14–15; 2 Peter 3:12).

Moved by the beauty and cry coming forth from the lives of His people, and clothed in the incense of their prayers, at the bidding of His Father who has prepared a wedding for His Son, Jesus will at last *return* (Psalm 45:8; Matthew 22:2). And the Wedding Supper of the Lamb will come, His Bride having kept first love burning and having made herself ready (Song of Solomon 3:11; Revelation 2:4; 19:7). As the song declares:

> From the ends of the earth, You'll hear our song
> Glory to the righteous one
> Every nation, every tribe, will be to You a spotless bride
> And this song that we now raise is hastening the day
> You will have Your inheritance
> Starting with my heart
> Desire of the nations, You will come to us.
> Hope of creation, You will come to us.
> Hallelujah, our Bridegroom is coming
> Hallelujah, He will reign[6]

And as His Word proclaims:

"Let us be glad and rejoice and give Him glory, for the marriage of the Lamb has come, and His wife has made herself ready." And to her it was granted to be arrayed in fine linen, clean and bright, for the fine linen is the righteous acts of the saints. Then he said to me, "Write: 'Blessed are those who are called to the marriage supper of the Lamb!'" And he said to me, "These are the true sayings of God."

Revelation 19:7–9

Make haste, my beloved, and be like a gazelle or a young stag on the mountains of spices.

Song of Solomon 8:14

"I, Jesus, have sent my angel to testify to you about these things for the churches. I am the root and the descendant of David, the bright morning star." The Spirit and the Bride say, "Come." And let the one who hears say, "Come." And let the one who is thirsty come; let the one who desires take the water of life without price. . . . He who testifies to these things says, "Surely I am coming soon." Amen. Come, Lord Jesus! The grace of the Lord Jesus be with all. Amen.

Revelation 22:16–17, 20–21 ESV

Jesus never starts a fire and walks away. He never awakens desire without tending to its flame. Wherever He finds in us even a smoldering wick of sincere love, He blows upon the embers—unwilling for it to be quenched (Isaiah 42:3). With a zeal that never wanes and a faithfulness older than the stars, He stands poised and ready to give the willing heart every grace and to fan our love into full fire again, and forever. He is the Keeper of the flame. He is the Author, Restorer and Preserver of our first love as we respond to Him.

Even with my mustard seed–sized faith in the beginning, I underestimated the jealousy of Jesus to enflame my heart with faith and love wherever it had diminished. His call to first love does not come as a burden of pressure for us to bear up under but a *promise of grace* to all who will partner and say *yes* to Him in the process. The Lord is zealous to revive our hearts where they need reviving. To reignite first-faith where unbelief has crept in. To restore innocent, pure believing, untainted by disappointment or disheartenment. To reignite first passion, unreserved and openhearted.

He spared nothing to redeem us, and He spares nothing to *keep* us and mature us in holy love. Why? Because *we are His.* Because He never changed His mind. Because the desires that He awakened us with are more real than we know. Because He took seriously the vows that we made to Him in our youth, or in our earlier days, and He always had every intention of strengthening us to keep them if we would partner with His grace (Psalm 76:11). Because what He did in the very beginning with us, awakening our love and drawing our desires to Himself, was not to be the high point but the *foretaste* of our future. Because the early stirrings He started in us individually were only the prophetic signs of the astounding future He has for us as His Church, His inheritance, His Bride. As His Word proclaims: "Eye has not seen, nor ear heard, nor have entered into the heart of man the things which God has prepared for those who love Him" (1 Corinthians 2:9).

He spared nothing to redeem us, and He spares nothing to keep us and mature us in holy love.

We have yet to begin in Him fully. The future before us, both as individuals and together as His people, is magnificent and breathtaking in its scope. He is going to bring us all the way forward into a mature people, radiant in love and blameless in holiness before Him. He renews first love in us and restores our souls because what we did and what we knew *at first* was only a glimpse of where this story is headed. It was only the initial flashes of the all-consuming fire that will characterize our hearts and lives by the end of the story. *We have truly only just begun.*

PRAYER

Jesus, open the eyes of my heart to see the splendid future You are bringing Your Bride into before Your return. Tenderize my heart by the wonder of it all and ignite faith in me to believe You will do it. I ask You to bring me forth into the fullness of love: a love in full maturity with all the first love *qualities until the very end, burning with the very same love that is in You, longing for Your return as a betrothed bride. Let me love You, Jesus, with this fiery love, until the end.*

STEPS FORWARD IN KEEPING FIRST LOVE

- Ask the Lord for grace and revelation by His Spirit to fully believe the victory He is bringing His Church into at the end of the age—and how He will cause your own heart and life to be caught up in that glorious victory.
- Make an appointment with a spouse or friend to talk about your current schedule. Listen to what the Holy Spirit wants you to prune in this season. Add, eliminate and reorder as needed to prioritize in your schedule the Word, worship, fasting and prayer.
- Set your heart before the Lord to zealously persist in ordering your life to be given to a lifestyle of prayer, where you seek to continually abide in His love and His Word, that your love would come into full, vibrant maturity and your passion for Him would be kept fervent until the day you see His face.

NOTES

Chapter 2 Returning to the Bridegroom Who Loved Us First

1. John Piper, "A Tender Word for Pharisees," Desiring God, February 16, 2014, https://www.desiringgod.org/messages/a-tender-word-to-pharisees/.
2. Augustus Toplady, "Rock of Ages, Cleft for Me," 1763, first published in *The Gospel Magazine*, 1775.
3. Piper, "A Tender Word for Pharisees."
4. Jon Thurlow, "I Want Your Heart," 2017, on *Different Story* (US: Forerunner Music).

Chapter 3 Embracing the Ache of Holy, Vulnerable Desire for God

1. C. S. Lewis, *Surprised by Joy* (San Francisco: HarperOne, 2017), 18, 72.
2. C. S. Lewis, *The Weight of Glory* (New York: Macmillan, 1949), 26.
3. A. W. Tozer, *The Pursuit of God* (Chicago: Moody Publishers, 2015), 23.

Chapter 4 Repenting of Unbelief and Recovering Confident Trust

1. G. K. Chesterton, *Orthodoxy* (Nashville: Sam Torode Book Arts, 2016), 56; originally published by Chesterton in 1908.

Chapter 5 Setting Our Hearts toward the Wilderness Pathway

1. Stephen Venable, "The Springs of Life," ACTS, April 30, 2015, http://www.actsresearch.global/resources/incense/communion-jesus/springs-life/.
2. Misty Edwards, "The Way of God Is the Wilderness."
3. I've taken liberty in rephrasing the Scripture to read as we would say it.
4. Misty Edwards, "Always on His Mind," 2005, on *Always on His Mind* (Forerunner Music).

5. C. S. Lewis, *Till We Have Faces* (Frankfurt am Main: Musaicum Books, 2017).

Chapter 6 Enduring God's Loving Chastening in Our Friendship with Jesus

1. Bob Sorge, *The Chastening of the Lord: The Forgotten Doctrine* (Grandview, MO: Oasis House, 2016), 122–123, 127–128.

2. For an extensive treatise on God's chastening, including how to understand the times that are the Lord's chastening in our lives and the times that are not, see *The Chastening of the Lord* by Bob Sorge.

3. Sorge, *Chastening of the Lord*, 35.

Chapter 7 Walking in Forgiving and Fervent Love for One Another

1. John Piper, "How to Live in History's Last Days," Desiring God, September 19, 2015, https://www.desiringgod.org/messages/how-to-live-in -historys-last-days/.

Chapter 8 Overcoming the Trouble of Accusation and Betrayal

1. Andrew Peterson, "Love Is a Good Thing," 2008, on *Resurrection Letters: Volume Two* (Centricity Music).

Chapter 9 Laying Hold of the Promise of Light, Love and Joy Together

1. David Sliker, *The Triumph of Beauty: The Glory of the Church at the End of the Age*, sermon at Forerunner Church, 2020.

Chapter 10 Burning with Unquenchable Love until He Comes

1. Samuel Whitefield, *It Must Be Finished: Making Sense of the Return of Jesus* (Kansas City, MO: OneKing Publishing, 2015), 150.

2. John Piper, *A Hunger for God: Desiring God through Fasting and Prayer* (Wheaton: Crossway Books, 1997), 84, 86.

3. Whitefield, *It Must Be Finished*, 150.

4. Whitefield, *It Must Be Finished*, 148.

5. Whitefield, *It Must Be Finished*, 153.

6. Ryan Kondo, "From the Ends of the Earth," 2013, on *Sing Your Praises* (US: Onething Live).

Dana Candler lives in Kansas City with her husband, Matthew, and their four children. She has been a senior leader at the International House of Prayer since its beginning in 1999. She serves as teaching faculty and the prayer director, together with Matt, at the International House of Prayer University. Additionally, she is an international speaker and the author of *Deep unto Deep*, *Entirety* and *Longing for His Return*. Her passion is to see the Church fully alive in a deep love for Jesus. Learn more at danacandler.com.